ADVANCE PI
FROM THIS DAY
RETHINKING THE CHRISTIAN WEDDING

"Kimberly Bracken Long writes a hopeful, compelling, and refreshing vision of Christian marriage with the recognition that a fancy wedding doesn't make a faithful marriage. Through historical, scriptural, theological, and practical considerations, she guides the reader toward the unfailing and unifying love of God that is the firm foundation of any marriage and life. Her forgiving, mutual, compassionate, and just vision cuts through contemporary anguish and debates about marriage and reestablishes the ground of hope in God. This book will stir your heart and mind to long for the wedding banquet feast to come when we take our seat and put our feet under God's Table."

—**LUKE POWERY**, Dean of Duke Chapel and
Associate Professor of Homiletics, Duke University,
and Author of *Dem Dry Bones: Preaching, Death, and Hope*

"I have performed hundreds of weddings in my thirty years of ministry, and never have I come across a book about weddings as sensible as this one. Kimberly Bracken Long has done her homework. This volume is well researched and down-to-earth: Serious scholarship that is not heavy, practical insight that is wiser than it is prescriptive, and personal testimony that is devoid of sentimentality. *From This Day Forward* is a treasure for pastors and couples who want an honest perspective on the wedding moment."

—**PETER W. MARTY**, Publisher, *The Christian Century*

"From Elvis serenading ceremonies, to Disney princess carriages, to intimate family gatherings, Kimberly Bracken Long follows the rituals of weddings as they weave through our history, lives, and faith. Long's formative voice wrests the theological richness from the extravagant events and the ravenous 'industry' that threatens to engulf our covenants. Easily accessible and deeply meaningful, *From This Day Forward* is a crucial resource for those who preside over services and those who enter into the wondrous promises of marriage."

—**CAROL HOWARD MERRITT**, Pastor and
Author of *Healing Spiritual Wounds*

"Kim Long's vision of marriage as holy work invites pastors and churches to reimagine marriage as a part of the church's mission. Her insights about Christian wedding practices, rooted in Scripture and the history of marriage, offer wise guidance to pastors in their work with couples preparing for a wedding and for married life."

—**RUTH MEYERS**, Dean of Academic Affairs
and Hodges-Haynes Professor of Liturgics,
Church Divinity School of the Pacific

"Long reminds us why celebrating and supporting marriages is part of the church's calling. She provides a wise and practical guide for pastors trying to navigate weddings with integrity and grace."

—**AMY PLANTINGA PAUW**, Henry P. Mobley Jr.
Professor of Doctrinal Theology, Louisville
Presbyterian Seminary

FROM THIS DAY FORWARD—
RETHINKING THE CHRISTIAN WEDDING

Also by Kimberly Bracken Long
from Westminster John Knox Press

The Eucharist Theology of the American Holy Fairs

Feasting on the Word Worship Companion:
Liturgies for Year A, Volume 1

Feasting on the Word Worship Companion:
Liturgies for Year A, Volume 2

Feasting on the Word Worship Companion:
Liturgies for Year B, Volume 1

Feasting on the Word Worship Companion:
Liturgies for Year B, Volume 2

Feasting on the Word Worship Companion:
Liturgies for Year C, Volume 1

Feasting on the Word Worship Companion:
Liturgies for Year C, Volume 2

Inclusive Marriage Services: A Wedding Sourcebook
(coedited with David Maxwell)

The Worshiping Body: The Art of Leading Worship

FROM THIS DAY FORWARD— RETHINKING THE CHRISTIAN WEDDING

KIMBERLY BRACKEN LONG

WESTMINSTER
JOHN KNOX PRESS
LOUISVILLE · KENTUCKY

First edition
Published by Westminster John Knox Press
Louisville, Kentucky

16 17 18 19 20 21 22 23 24 25—10 9 8 7 6 5 4 3 2 1

Scripture quotations are from the New Revised Standard Version of the Bible, copyright © 1989 by the Division of Christian Education of the National Council of the Churches of Christ in the U.S.A., and are used by permission. Excerpt from "The Country of Marriage," by Wendell Berry copyright © 1973 by Wendell Berry, from *The Country of Marriage.* Reprinted by permission of Counterpoint. Excerpt from a sermon "Marriage Matters . . . Why?" by Brian Ellison is reprinted by permission of the author. Excerpt of a prayer from *Lutheran Book of* Worship copyright © 1978 Lutheran Book of Worship admin. Augsburg Fortress. Reproduced by permission. Marriage blessing from *Evangelical Lutheran Worship,* Pew Edition (Minneapolis: Augsburg Fortress, 2006) is used by permission of the publisher. Excerpts from Kimberly Bracken Long and David Maxwell, eds., *Inclusive Marriage Services: A Wedding Sourcebook* (Louisville, KY: Westminster John Knox Press, 2015) are used by permission of the publisher. Portion of a eucharistic prayer written by David Gambrell is used by permission of the author. Excerpts adapted from *The Companion to the* Book of Common Worship, ed. Peter C. Bower (Louisville, KY: Geneva Press, 2003) are used by permission of the publisher. Excerpts from *The Book of Common Worship* (Louisville, KY: Westminster/John Knox Press, 1993) are used by permission of the publisher. Excerpts from Standing Commission on Liturgy and Music, *Liturgical Resources 1: I Will Bless You and You Will Be a Blessing,* rev. ed. (New York: Church Publishing, 2015) are used by permission of the publisher.

Book design by Erika Lundbom-Krift
Cover design by Mark Abrams
Cover image design Freepik.com

Library of Congress Cataloging-in-Publication Data

Names: Long, Kimberly Bracken, author.
Title: From this day forward-rethinking the Christian wedding / Kimberly
  Bracken Long.
Description: Louisville, KY : Westminster John Knox Press, 2016.
Identifiers: LCCN 2015047265 | ISBN 9780664239305 (alk. paper)
Subjects: LCSH: Marriage--Religious aspects--Christianity. | Marriage. |
  Weddings.
Classification: LCC BV835 .L665 2016 | DDC 265/.5--dc23 LC record available at https://
lccn.loc.gov/2015047265

Most Westminster John Knox Press books are available at special quantity discounts when purchased in bulk by corporations, organizations, and special-interest groups. For more information, please e-mail SpecialSales@wjkbooks.com.

Two weddings.

One large, one small. One rainy, one sunny. One with dancing, one with fireworks. Both brides wore white. Both grooms adored their brides. And I adored both grooms, because I was their mother. Truth be told, I loved their sweethearts, too. And, as if that were not enough, I was privileged to preside at both weddings.

It's not often that a scholar begins an academic pursuit only to find her own life circumstances colliding—joyfully—with her work. Somewhere around the time that I began a sabbatical to study marriage, my older son announced his engagement. Somewhere around the time that I began to put words to paper, my younger son pledged to spend his life with the one human being he loves best.

They saved me. They saved you, too, from reading a book too sharply cynical regarding the nuptial fuss, too rigidly insistent on what the church has to do with it all, and not nearly aware enough of the joyful chaos that surrounds even the simplest of weddings.

It seems natural, then, that this book would be dedicated to these four, with my prayers for a life full of blessing and, of course, with my love.

For
Nate and Katie, m. July 15, 2012
Dan and Sallie, m. May 24, 2014

CONTENTS

ACKNOWLEDGMENTS

I began this work during a yearlong leave made possible by the generous support of a Sabbatical Grant for Researchers from the Louisville Institute and a Lilly Theological Research Grant from the Association of Theological Schools. I am grateful to Columbia Theological Seminary for making it possible to be released from my duties for an entire academic year.

During that sabbatical year, a number of pastors around the country convened groups of ministers for conversation and provided warm hospitality. I am grateful to Scott Anderson, Adam Copeland, Marci Glass, David Hawkins, Maggi Henderson, Kim Hulen, and Frank Lewis for their help and enthusiasm for the project. Felicia Glass-Wilcox, owner of the Chapel of Love in the Mall of America; Charlotte Eulette, director of the Celebrant Foundation and Institute in Montclair, New Jersey; and Charolette Richards, proprietor of A Little White Wedding Chapel in Las Vegas; graciously gave of their time in allowing me to interview them about their work.

It is impossible to name all of the students at Columbia Theological Seminary who contributed to the shaping of this book. The members of a combined DMin/MDiv class, Sexuality, Marriage, and the 21st Century Church, gave invaluable help as I was working through the ideas represented in this book. Kelly Couch, Andrew Daugherty, Daniel Hagmaier, Barbara Johnson, Noe Juarez, Delesslyn Killebrew, Kathryn Lamon,

Olive Mahabir, Christy McMillin-Goodwin, John Menefee, Dominique Robinson, and Meiying Shi—thank you for your openness, honesty, creativity, and patience with me as I found my way.

So many colleagues at Columbia have offered their encouragement and support during the five years I worked on this project. The librarians must come first! Mary Martha Riviere and Griselda Lartey were ever helpful, and Erica Durham saved the day on more occasions than I can count, especially when I was several states away and needed help. Erica also assisted me by transcribing the many interviews I conducted. Kim Clayton cheered me on and shared pastoral wisdom. Martha Moore-Keish, Kathleen O'Connor, Christine Yoder, Beth Johnson, and Catherine Gunsalus González gave invaluable help on various drafts, doing their best to ensure that I did not embarrass myself with any biblical, historical, or theological assertions. Any errors are, of course, all mine.

I am grateful to members of the Liturgical Language and Liturgy and Culture seminars at the North American Academy of Liturgy for their consideration of my work along the way. Opportunities to present my work at Decatur Presbyterian Church in Decatur, Georgia, a conference in Chicago of the Covenant Network of Presbyterians, and classes taught at the Montreat Worship and Music Conference helped to further my thinking. Thanks especially to Julia Wharff Piermont and Buz Wilcoxon for their thoughtful responses. I owe a debt of gratitude to Ted Wardlaw, president of Austin Presbyterian Theological Seminary, for inviting me to give the Jones Lectures at that institution's Midwinter Lectures in February 2015; not only did the deadline help me make significant progress, but the positive responses I received there encouraged me immensely.

In the final throes of preparing the manuscript, Julie Erkel Hagee and Melissa Tidwell gave invaluable help. Thank you.

Portions of chapter 4 were published as "Practicing the Scales of Love: Rethinking Christian Marriage," in *Presbyterian Outlook*. A version of chapter 6 appeared as "Marriage and the Church's Mission" in *Liturgy*.

I am grateful, of course, to my editor at Westminster John Knox Press, David Maxwell, who has a knack for keeping me on track and exhibits endless patience with my well-honed talent for procrastination.

Finally, thank you to my kids for getting married, and for doing it so well. And thank you, my beloved Tom, for everything.

Chapter 1

THE STATE OF THE UNION

With this ring I thee wed,
with my body I thee worship,
and with all my worldly goods I thee endow.

Caught up in a heady mix of passion, faith, and hope, standing before my congregation on a Sunday morning, I repeated these age-old words to my beloved some two decades ago. I had just vowed to be loving and faithful through every circumstance for the rest of our lives. I had no idea what I was doing.

I daresay no one really knows what she or he is getting into when speaking such rash words of commitment. On one hand, taking wedding vows is an ordinary enough thing to do. Lots of people get married. And yet to marry is to enter into unknown territory; to speak vows is to take the first step into a common-place mystery.

For Christians, the mystery of marriage is all tied up with the mystery of faith. Every earthly wedding feast, however sumptuous or simple, anticipates the wedding feast of the Lamb that

1

celebrates the marriage of heaven and earth. And some marriages, by the grace of God, give us a glimpse of the coming reign of God when the whole creation will be overwhelmed with love.

And yet . . . we are aware, whether we are married or not, that as beautiful and blessed as marriage can be, it is a fragile institution, because the human beings who take part in it are fickle and flawed. Whether we know it from our own lives, or from those of our friends, or from the news, we are aware of how complicated marriage is these days. Being Christian does not protect us from the complexities of the human heart or the realities of human sin, nor does it excuse us from taking part in responding to changes in attitudes and actions of the larger society.

This book is an attempt to speak to the American church in a time of extraordinary cultural change. The first years of the twenty-first century have brought seismic shifts to the institution of marriage, following dramatic changes in attitudes regarding marriage and family life over the last half century or so. To varying degrees, churches are asking questions about the meaning of marriage, the church's role in the weddings of Christians and non-Christians alike, and how to navigate faithfully through the swift currents and shifting tides of American life. In order to explore Christian understandings of marriage, we will consider the history of marriage in human society and in the church; the biblical texts that contribute to theologies of marriage; and the theology and practice of wedding services. We will begin by taking a look at the landscape of marriage in the United States.

IS MARRIAGE OUT OF DATE?

Now that more than half of Americans are single, some may wonder whether marriage is becoming a thing of the past.[1] In 1950, ninety of every one thousand unmarried women tied the knot. By contrast, only thirty-one of every thousand single women got married in 2011, representing a 66 percent decline in the marriage rate, indicating that marriage is becoming a thing of the past.[2]

For one thing, people are waiting longer to get married. Today the average age of women who marry (for the first time) is twenty-seven; the average age for men is twenty-nine. Almost a third of women and over 40 percent of men wait until they are at least thirty to get married.[3] Marriage has not gone out of style, as some social critics feared, but it is "no longer the central institution that organizes people's lives."[4] More and more people choose cohabitation over marriage—at least for a while—either as a way to test out life with a potential marriage partner or to enjoy love, sex, and companionship without making a legal, lifelong commitment.

Intimate relationships often take a different course than they used to. When author W. Hodding Carter's girlfriend blurted, "Let's get a dog," as they were eating their morning pancakes, it caught him by surprise. Carter knew that getting a dog wasn't just about acquiring a pet. Getting a dog meant taking their relationship to a new level. "Getting 'the dog,'" he knows, "is a classic early step, falling soundly between the first kiss and ordering a copy of *What to Expect When You're Expecting*." They'd been a couple for about a year and had lived in the same apartment for a few months. He wasn't opposed to taking the next step but thought that he needed a couple of weeks to think through the implications. Four hours later, he and Lisa had a dog.[5]

Only a generation has passed since the usual course of things looked something like this:

You start going out.
You become an item.
You get engaged.
You get married.

You move in together.
You have sex.
You have a baby.
You have another baby.
You buy a house.
You get a dog.[6]

Now, it seems, the dog almost always comes first, right after moving in together.

In fact, two-thirds of couples who decide to get married are living together already. This used to mean that couples were more likely to divorce, but researchers find that is no longer the case for couples who have married since the mid-1990s.[7] More recent studies show that divorce rates fall dramatically when the age of either cohabitation or marriage is delayed. Sociologist Arielle Kuperburg found that people who moved in together or got married at age eighteen were twice as likely to divorce as those who waited until age twenty-three (60 percent versus 30 percent). Over the last fifty years, the rate of cohabitation has jumped by 900 percent. In 1996, 2.9 million couples lived together before marriage; in 2012, that number was 7.8 million. Furthermore, two-thirds of couples who married in 2012 had lived together for at least two years. Not surprisingly, then, a USA Today/Gallup poll in 2007 showed that only 27 percent of Americans disapprove of cohabitation.[8] Given such statistics, it is safe to say that some of those cohabitating couples are Christians; certainly many of the couples who come to pastors' offices to discuss their upcoming nuptials go home together that night.

Although there is plenty of evidence that many people still want to get married, some have decided that marriage is an outdated institution that puts unrealistic expectations on contemporary couples. Still others say that watching someone else go through a divorce is enough to swear them off marriage for good. They are not avoiding marriage because they are afraid of commitment; they are afraid of divorce. Furthermore, people are living longer. Lifelong monogamy seems less and less realistic, and there is considerably less legal and financial mess when cohabiting couples split, especially if they've kept their bank accounts separate.

EDUCATION, POVERTY, RACE, AND MARRIAGE

While some studies seem to indicate that marriage is in decline in this country, a recent study by the Pew Research Center shows that the number of marriages increased in the United States in 2012. One significant factor emerges, however; people with college degrees accounted for 87 percent of the increase in newly married adults between 2011 and 2012.[9]

For Jonathan Rauch, a fellow at the Brookings Institution, this is cause for concern. "Marriage is thriving among people with four-year college diplomas," he says, "but the further down you go on the educational and economic totem pole, the worse it's doing. There's a growing danger that marriage, with all its advantages for stability, income, and child well-being, will look like a gated community for the baccalaureate class, with ever-shrinking working-class participation."[10]

Education plays an important role in marriage among those in the middle class as well as those living in poverty. The number of women who earn a college degree is rising, and these women are looking for equally educated and employable marriage partners in a pool that is steadily shrinking. Women who graduated from high school used to be able to marry men with college degrees, but these days they are less likely to marry at all. These women, especially white women, are more likely than other women to cohabit, marry, divorce, and cohabit again. It is not yet clear whether marriage patterns in the middle class will turn out to look like those of upper-class people or their lower-class counterparts.[11] Meanwhile, women who have attained a high level of education are now more likely to get married and stay married. Divorce rates are falling among well-educated couples but rising for everyone else.

Views on marriage and cohabitation, then, are not based solely on moral convictions or religious beliefs. Levels of education, social class, and economic realities have a great deal to do with whether people marry in the first place, as well as the success or failure of their marriages. Over the last twenty years or so, marriage has nearly disappeared in poorer communities. People whose incomes fall in the lower third of the population experience greater rates of unemployment, substance abuse, and imprisonment—particularly among men—which leads to an increasing disparity between men and women, making them less likely to marry.[12] As one commentator has put it, "The real trend is that marriage is for richer, not poorer."[13]

Poverty is, in fact, a significant contributing factor to lower marriage rates in the United States. Potential mates for women who live in economically disadvantaged neighborhoods are likely to have lower levels of education and irregular employment opportunities. Lower-earning men marry less frequently and divorce more often than men who earn better wages. Over the last several decades, as job opportunities for less-educated men declined, marriage rates also fell.[14]

Sociologist Stephanie Coontz and economist Nancy Folbre found that mothers with few financial resources are apt to live in poor neighborhoods where possible marriage partners tend to be poorly educated and employed only sporadically. These men are less likely to marry and, if they do, divorce is more probable than for higher-earning men. Marriage rates fall as incomes decline. Furthermore, when men are convicted of nonviolent crimes and sentenced to prison, they are less likely to marry or to be able to secure stable employment after their release.[15]

It is impossible to overlook race when considering the effects of poverty on marriage. In his controversial book, provocatively titled *Is Marriage For White People?*, Ralph Richard Banks explains that African American women across social classes often do not marry because so many black men are incarcerated, lack education, or are unemployed or otherwise economically disadvantaged. Twice as many African American women as men earn a college degree, making them less likely to marry than women of other races. Of those college-educated black women who do marry, more than half are wed to men who are less educated. Furthermore, while African American women do marry across class lines, they are far less likely to marry across race lines.[16]

The connection between marriage and childbearing is also in flux in the United States. As one study by the Pew Research Center suggests, for adults born after 1980, "these social institutions are becoming delinked and differently valued."[17] For these "millennials," parenthood is more important than marriage. The rise in the average age of marriage is accompanied by a rise in out-of-wedlock births. In 2008, 51 percent of children born to millennials were born to parents who were not married, in contrast to only 39 percent to parents of the same age in 1997. At the same time, however, fewer young adults are becoming parents; in 2010, only 36 percent of women between the ages of eighteen and twenty-nine had borne children.[18] Still, most young adults look forward to being parents—even if they don't necessarily anticipate getting married.[19]

Yet another phenomenon contributes to the complex picture of marriage in America. One in five divorces among people married for the first time happens within the first five years.[20] Often dubbed "starter marriages," these unions last five years or less and produce no children. These couples do not marry with the intention of divorcing; more often than not, they think they are marrying for life. "A starter marriage isn't a whim or a fantasy or a misbegotten affair," explains Pamela Paul, author of *The Starter Marriage and the Future of Matrimony*, "it's a real marriage . . . bound together by love, personal belief, state law, and, often, religious oath. A starter marriage doesn't *feel* like one when you're engaged or when you're inside it. It is charged with all the hope, expectations, and dreams that inspire almost all marriages."[21] While the idea of a starter marriage is shocking to some, others argue that the starter marriage is useful in teaching people what not to do so that they can eventually enjoy a successful second marriage.[22]

Still other social realities raise new questions for society at large as well as the church. According to the Pew Research Center, marriage is on the rise between people of different religions, as well as different races and ethnic groups. Nearly four in ten people who wed in 2010 married a spouse from a different religious group, roughly twice the number of those who did so before 1960. Of all adults married in the United States between 2010 and 2014, 18 percent are in marriages between a Christian and a person with no religious affiliation. Furthermore, almost half of cohabiting couples are partners of different faiths.[23]

Pew studies also show that record numbers are marrying people of a different race. Roughly 15 percent of people who wed in 2010 married someone of a different race or ethnic group. Statistics vary depending on race, gender, levels of education, and economic stability, so the picture is multivalent, and states where the intermarriage rate is above 20 percent are all west of the Mississippi.[24]

DIVORCE IN AMERICA

We have heard for a long time that one out of every two marriages in America ends in divorce, leading pundits and pulpiteers to bemoan the loss of family values. Although not all researchers agree on that figure, we can certainly say that divorce has become more commonplace—and less stigmatized—in recent decades. One reason for this, as sociologist Andrew Cherlin observes, is that Americans are as committed to the idea of individual freedom as they are to marriage:

> The United States is unique among nations in its strong support for marriage, on one hand, and its postmodern penchant for self-expression and personal growth, on the other hand. You can find other Western countries where marriage is strong, such as Italy, where few children are born outside of marriage and relatively few people live together without marrying, and you can find Western countries with highly individualistic values, such as Sweden, where marriage and cohabitation are virtually indistinguishable. But only in the United States can you find both. [25]

The United States, then, has one of the highest levels of marriage among Western countries—and one of the highest divorce rates, too. Of course, the statistics on divorce tell different stories, depending on who is doing the analyzing and the methods used. It seems, however, that because so many are delaying marriage, divorce is less common among younger people. At the same time, it is becoming more common for long-term marriages to break up when the partners reach middle age.[26]

Given these patterns of less frequent marriage, more frequent divorce, the prevalence of cohabitation, and the rising number of children born to unmarried parents, it would seem that the state of marriage is worse than ever. Yet the *quality* of marriage is, for some, better than ever. Marriage is less confining for women, who are more autonomous than they were fifty years ago. Psychological researcher Eli Finkel makes the case that marriages on average are weaker than they used to be, but that "the *best* marriages today are much stronger, in terms of both satisfaction and personal well-being."[27] As we shall see in chapter 3, Americans today have expectations of marriage that would have been inconceivable at any other time in history.

Those expectations are so high that experts like Finkel claim that people can "achieve an unprecedentedly high level of marital quality—but only if they are able to invest a great deal of time and energy in their partnership." And yet, he argues, economic trends that have led to greater inequality over the last several decades, resulting in unemployment or people managing more than one job, make it even more difficult for middle- and lower-class Americans to devote the time and energy required to maintain a strong marriage.[28] Clearly the picture of marriage in this country is a complex mixture of changing social attitudes, economic realities, and class issues.

SAME-GENDER MARRIAGE AND THE PUBLIC DEBATE

Meanwhile, changes regarding same-sex marriage have swept the United States far more quickly than either its proponents or its detractors could have predicted. The repeal of the Defense of Marriage Act, or DOMA, in 2013 led to the legalization of same-sex marriage in a number of states, and the country watched the wave of change that culminated in the June 26, 2015, decision of the Supreme Court that affirmed that the U.S. Constitution guarantees a right to same-sex marriage. Across the theological spectrum, churches are considering how to respond. In some cases, denominational polity is changing; in others, churches continue to prohibit clergy to preside at such weddings, putting ministers in an awkward spot as they seek to be faithful to their ordination vows while tending to the pastoral needs of their flocks.

As laws change and conversations become more open, we hear moving stories of same-gender couples who are marrying after years of sharing life together. Forty-six years after they fell in love, Lewis Duckett and Billy Jones got married. Dr. Jones, a psychiatrist, was deployed to Vietnam not long after they met, and the two wrote letters almost every day, using code and changing gender pronouns so that no one would know they were gay. Eventually they moved in together and adopted a child, a son, when he was just three weeks old. That son is now grown, and they are the proud grandparents of a little girl. In October 2013, Mr. Duckett and Dr. Jones were married in Riverside Church in New York, solemnifying—and making legal—the life they have shared for four and a half decades.[29] The following year, Vivian Boyack and Alice "Nonie" Dubes, both nonagenarians, were married in their church in Davenport, Iowa, celebrating a relationship they have shared for over seventy years.[30]

The public debate surrounding same-sex marriage has surfaced long-held assumptions about marriage. When, for example, the U.S. Supreme Court heard arguments regarding California's Proposition 8 (a statewide referendum that would eliminate same-sex marriage), it became clear that even when it comes to public policy, traditional Judeo-Christian ideas influence the discussion. The attorney defending Proposition 8 argued that marriage should be defined as being between a man and a woman because society is interested in responsible procreation. Justices Elena Kagan and Stephen Breyer challenged this notion, pointing out that not all heterosexual couples are able to procreate, and therefore this should not be an obstacle to the marriage of people of the same sex. The attorney responded that redefining marriage as a "genderless institution will sever its abiding connection to its historic traditional procreative purposes," shifting the purpose and definition "away from the raising of children and to the emotional needs and desires of adults, of adult couples."[31] Although Kagan countered that the attorney's line of reasoning would lead to the banning of marriage for anyone over fifty-five—since they would be highly unlikely to bear any children—the attorney insisted that there is a "marital norm" that is based on the procreation and raising of children. Reflecting on the exchange, sociologist Rosemary

Joyce expressed her astonishment that a legal argument would assert that marriage has a consistent, stable history; there is no "age-old definition of marriage," no matter what the counsel claimed. "To an anthropologist," she remarks, "that sounds remarkably quaint. Whose age-old definition?"[32]

Whose definition, indeed? One of the gifts of the public conversation around same-sex marriage is that it has spurred churches to ask deeper questions about the nature of marriage in general. We are beginning to explore the history of marriage (both in and out of the church), to consider what constitutes a faithful theology of marriage, and to engage the biblical witness while taking seriously contemporary life as well as pastoral concerns.

A GOLDEN AGE OF MARRIAGE?

Although there is a considerable amount of hand-wringing these days about the state of marriage in the United States, there is a sense in which none of this is new. Social critics in ancient Greece decried the moral failures of wives, and the Romans complained about high divorce rates.[33] In sixteenth-century Geneva, John Calvin and other pastors complained that upper-class couples were divorcing and remarrying at alarming rates.[34] Genevans were enjoying casual sex, living together without being married, and keeping concubines,[35] all of which drove Calvin to insist on firmer laws and a more fulsome theology of marriage. Early settlers in America started bemoaning the loss of family values as soon as they stepped onto shore. It seems that there never really has been a "golden age of marriage."[36]

Yet whatever the time and place, Christians are called to respond to the challenges of the day. How shall contemporary Christians speak to the current social context while honoring the lives of real Christians living in the real world? In order to do that, we need to take a step back and consider what marriage is, how Scripture informs our understanding of marriage, what theological affirmations we can make about the nature of marriage, how our marriage liturgies express those convictions, and what role the clergy and the entire church community play in the marriage of Christians.

HOW THIS BOOK CAME ABOUT

When I began in ordained ministry, I quickly discovered how woefully unprepared I was to talk to anyone about getting married, or being married, or whether to keep being married. After gamely subjecting couples to the requisite premarital counseling, I would wonder what in the world I was doing and who decided that this should be part of my job. Although I could not have articulated it at the time, I realize now that I had plenty of therapeutic resources at my disposal, but few theological ones, for talking about the meaning of marriage. Often I found myself smiling congenially through wedding ceremonies for people I barely knew—despite the sessions we endured together— and the receptions that followed where I would inevitably be seated with an assortment of grandmothers, next-door neighbors, and all of the other people the couple didn't know what to do with. There were, of course, those rare occasions when I was privileged to preside at the wedding of parishioners or family members I knew and loved. But most of the time, I found the duties surrounding nuptials to be demoralizing and exhausting.

When I began teaching seminary students about weddings, I realized how little material I had to draw on. I could find histories of marriage and sociological studies; there were works of Roman Catholic and Orthodox sacramental theology. Here and there I found a helpful article or essay, as well as collections of historic marriage liturgies. It occurred to me that many ministers are credentialed to preside at weddings, but few of us receive much theological, liturgical, or practical training to do so. I decided to see what I could discover.

Over the past several years I have talked with groups of ministers across the country about their experiences with weddings and their insights into Christian marriage. My own students at Columbia Theological Seminary—single, married, divorced, engaged—have lent me their wisdom as well. Various theologians, historians, sociologists, and commentators have accompanied me on the journey. I have interviewed wedding entrepreneurs, listened to Elvis croon couples down the aisle, and learned from the experiences and wisdom of gay and lesbian friends and acquaintances. During the course of my research, I enjoyed the privilege of presiding at the weddings of both of my sons. This work is challenging, stimulating, personal, and public. What follows is my best effort at contributing to a conversation about marriage that might further the work of the contemporary church as we seek to proclaim the good news of Jesus Christ.

While I would like to think I could write a book that would be helpful to all American Christian churches, I know that is impossible. I write as a white, well-educated, financially stable woman. I have been Presbyterian all my life, am ordained as a minister of the Word and Sacrament (or teaching elder) in the Presbyterian Church (U.S.A.), and teach at a Presbyterian seminary. While my work in the church has been ecumenically informed, and my teaching career has enabled me to be in conversation with students from a wide range of denominations and traditions, my approach is decidedly Reformed. I understand that the issues facing the Roman Catholic and Orthodox churches are in some ways different from those facing the Protestant churches. While some of what I discuss in this book may be of help or interest to African American, Korean, or Latino/a churches, I cannot legitimately speak to questions that are particular to those contexts. Finally, I write as one who is convinced that marriage is between two people, whoever they are and whomever they love. Others have made the case for same-sex marriage clearly and compellingly, and I will not rehearse their work here.[37] I will, however, approach the subject of marriage as a relationship and an institution that is legally available for all people and worthy of blessing in the church.

It takes a combination of hubris and humility to write a book about marriage. As Margaret Farley has said, "Rhetoric about marriage and family needs to be realistic and cautious—neither too high-flying nor too skeptical."[38] It is a daunting subject and, in the end, a mystery. While this book is the result of several years of study and innumerable conversations, it is also borne of my own experience. I have been married twice and divorced once. I believe deeply in the gift of marriage and know something of both its challenges and its graces. Being married has taught me a great deal about the nature of self-giving love and the miracle of forgiveness; in marriage I have seen the love of Christ made present in ways I could never have imagined. In spite of my limitations—personal, pastoral, and academic—I hope that this book will offer insights for those contemplating marriage, provide theological perspective for those doing the hard work of staying married, and give a framework of redemption and hope for those whose marriages have ended. The body of Christ need not be a place of secrecy or shame when it comes to marriage but rather a place of abundant life.

THE SHAPE OF THE BOOK

This book emerged as a result of trying to answer one essential question: Should the church get out of the wedding business? It is a question that I was once tempted to answer with a resounding yes. In chapter 2, I describe the source of the question and lay out the various ways people have answered it. In the end, I argue that the church needs to back away from the *wedding* business but stay in the *marriage* business. The landscape has changed over the last twenty centuries, however, and today's church needs to consider what that means.

In order to rethink the church's views of marriage and its involvement in weddings, I offer a brief history of marriage in chapter 3. Drawing on the work of sociologists and historians, I trace the ways people got married, and their reasons for doing so, over several centuries. The story of the church's involvement in marriage, while certainly intersecting with the overall historical arc, is told separately. Furthermore, it must be said that the story of marriage as I tell it is primarily a Euro-American story. I describe patterns that Americans both inherited and formed and reflect on an institution that was largely unavailable to people who were enslaved. The history of marriage among African American slaves is largely undocumented, and there is little written evidence regarding their patterns of courtship. Furthermore, the policies of individual slave owners determined whether formal unions among enslaved people were encouraged or even tolerated. Spouses could belong to different owners, and unlike the stories we hear today, property played little role in the choice of a partner.[39]

Understanding something of the evolution of thought in both the civil and ecclesial realms leads us to ask what Scripture says about marriage. In chapter 4 I discuss the basic "canon" of texts on marriage—particularly those that appear in marriage liturgies—and suggest strategies for interpreting difficult texts, holding texts in conversation with one another, and expanding the range of biblical passages in order to enlarge our understanding of what it means to be Christian and be married. This discussion of Scripture leads to the central claim of the book: marriage between Christians is best understood within an eschatological framework that draws on biblical notions of right relationship and is nourished by particular Christian practices, such as forgiveness, mutual self-giving, and hospitality.

The work of the first four chapters comes to bear in chapter 5, where we discuss the wedding service itself. Here I offer theological commentary on each element of the service and insights into what makes a marriage liturgy deeply faithful, broadly inclusive, and sensitive to various pastoral concerns. Chapter 5 also focuses on such practical details as music in weddings and how to get along with wedding planners. The final chapter explores how marriage might be part of the church's mission—before, during, and after the wedding—and urges the church toward more faithful responses to those who are divorcing or divorced. Two appendixes offer suggested scriptural passages for reading and preaching at weddings and a list of especially appropriate hymns and songs.

There are several things I am not doing in this book. I am not questioning monogamy. I am not arguing that being married is better than being single. I do not discuss important pastoral issues such as working with blended families, divorced parents, or cross-cultural marriage. There is important work to be done there, but it is beyond the scope of this volume.

This work has convinced me that the church has something to say about marriage, both for those who profess Christ and for those who do not. We offer a vision of marriage that is life-giving—one in which couples practice forgiveness as a daily habit, value the interests of the other above one's own in an economy of mutuality, and seek to be agents of compassion and justice to those around them. I hope that this book will help us lean into that vision with energy and love.

Chapter 2

SHOULD THE CHURCH GET OUT OF THE WEDDING BUSINESS?

"I'D RATHER DO TEN FUNERALS THAN ONE WEDDING." THE STATE-ment is so common among ministers that it has become cliché, though it might seem counterintuitive. Why would anyone pre-fer a season of mourning over one of joy? The answer is always the same: at a funeral, you proclaim what is at the heart of the faith, the ultimate depth and wonder of the gospel. At a wed-ding . . . well, not so much. These days, weddings—even church weddings—can seem to be about everything *but* the heart of the faith.

While researching Christian weddings, I traveled across the country, interviewing pastors from a wide range of com-munities and contexts. Their stories sounded very much the same. Ministers are tired of feeling like functionaries, cogs in a wedding machine that is so big it barely acknowledges their presence. "I remember the first time I bought a pickup," one Minnesota pastor said. "Everybody I knew said, 'You have a pickup now! I can use you for hauling my garbage to the dump this weekend.' When I got to be a minister, it was, 'Hey, you can do my wedding!'"

They told stories about couples whose desire for a church wedding was shaped by what they'd seen on television or at the movies. "Sometimes I think if I worked in an ugly building, I would enjoy [weddings] more," said one pastor in a large southern city. "But we have this large, Gothic, beautiful facility. . . . It's amazing how many weddings we do because people say, 'Isn't this a pretty place?'"

Some pastors described encountering couples who would submit to the minister's requirements of premarital and church attendance simply to earn the right to walk down a center aisle; in other cases, people joined the church so they could dodge the church's fees for nonmembers. Still others were asked to officiate at weddings because of the location of their churches. In one small town in West Virginia, couples will get a license at the courthouse and then walk down the street looking for a minister. "We are the first church," said one pastor. "Frank is the next church. Then Bob." The county courthouse is only one thing that draws couples. "Sometimes folk will come in between whatever activities they are doing at the racetrack," reported another minister. Since the racetrack is such a popular destination, people want to get married while they are there.

In large cities and small towns, pastors wonder over and over why they are spending their Friday nights and Saturday afternoons presiding over rehearsals and weddings for people who have little or no connection to the church and are not interested in one—all for an honorarium that is less than the limousine driver is being paid. The concerns of these ministers are not mercenary—but it becomes clear that participating in weddings has very little to do with Christian ministry, and they begin wondering just what it is they are doing, and why.

Many pastors raise questions regarding the relationship between their ecclesial and legal roles. Is there a conflict between being a servant of the church and an agent of the state? Should they sign marriage licenses at all? In some cases, couples want their wedding to be blessed by God and witnessed by a community of faith; in other cases, they simply need a minister from central casting to meet them at the botanical garden or on the beach.

Many pastors described a significant disconnect between their own expectations of what happens during a marriage service and what preparations are required and those of couples seeking to be married. Most require some form of premarital counseling; in some cases, it leads to a fruitful relationship between the couple and the pastor. Occasionally, couples will eventually join the church where they are married. At other times, however, pastors' interactions with the bride- and groom-to-be were less satisfying. "I used to require premarital counseling," said one minister, "and they would come and sit and go through the motions. I got tired of wasting my time on that. . . . I hate saying it, you get couples that come to you if they are not from the church and you can almost guarantee that they are going to lie to you. Say what you want to hear so they can get married." More than one minister described such disillusionment.

Not all ministers are so despairing. There are pastors who preside joyfully at weddings and do them well. They cultivate relationships with couples and engender connections with the wider church community. While most admit that the whole process is more gratifying when they know the couples, or the ones marrying are part of the life of their congregations (or both), there are some who appreciate the process of working through questions of faith with seekers or disaffected Christians. Often ministers see weddings as an opportunity for evangelism. For some, that means encouraging people to join the church. For others, however, it simply means sharing the good news. As one pastor put it, evangelism is "to talk about the faithfulness of God through all the things of our life. That's not just for the couple. That's for everyone who is there bringing all sorts of stuff with them . . . to talk about the steadfast love of God."

For some pastors, simply having an opportunity to talk about faith is enough. "I did a lot of weddings of people not connected with the church," one St. Louis pastor told me. "To me that was an opportunity to explore faith with them. They want to get married here, okay, that gives me the right to ask you questions, to pose questions about where God is in your life and why you want to get married in the church. Why does that matter? What difference does it make? Over the years I have had some really interesting conversations with people. Although not many of them join the church, I've discovered that when it came time for a funeral or some other connection, they tended to think of us as their church, whether or not they were official members." There is a missional aspect to participating in weddings.

One Minnesota pastor explained the reasons for saying yes to eight weddings in one summer. "So many people have fallen away from the church. Maybe they just got bored with it. Maybe they didn't have a bad experience. Maybe they just grew up and all they remember was a boring preacher droning on and on and once they got old enough, they didn't want any more to do with it. Maybe their parents forced them to go and they don't like the church. I want to be that person that says, hey, church can be really cool. I still want church to be that place where you feel free and safe to struggle with your faith, even if it means doing a wedding for someone who might not come back."

Two West Virginia pastors described similar attitudes. "What do you do when the church becomes the one saying no, no, no?" said one. "I feel like all those people who call," said another, "are all people I am called in some way to love, whether I say yes or no to the wedding, if they are inside or outside of the church. Especially if they are outside of the church. I am very concerned that we are closing doors."

I give thanks for those who have developed thoughtful approaches and discovered deep joy in this part of their pastoral vocation. Yet so many continue to struggle with questions of what they are doing, under whose auspices, and why. Some have given up trying to come to terms with it all; others labor on with a vague sense of just trying to accomplish something good. Still others decide—either individually or in conjunction with their congregations—to concentrate on blessing the marriages of believing Christians and forgo the privilege of signing marriage licenses. It seems evident that questions abound for churches and their pastors.

BEYOND THE CHURCH DOORS: VEGAS AND DISNEY

Not everyone, of course, gets married in the church. How might the work of other wedding entrepreneurs inform the questions that arise for pastors and congregations? In order to get a sense of what people outside the church were thinking and doing, I decided to investigate beyond the boundaries of church and academy.

My first stop was Las Vegas, home of no fewer than fifty wedding chapels. The day began at the Clark County Marriage License Bureau, where hopeful couples snaked their way along a roped pathway that would eventually take them to a county clerk. It could have been the Department of Motor Vehicles, but the licenses they sought would open to them not just the roadways but the most treacherous, and potentially rewarding, journey of their lives: marriage.

Outside, I perched on a stone wall to talk to anyone who was willing. I met the mother of an eighteen-year-old son and his very pregnant soon-to-be bride. They were living with her, and three days earlier she had half-jokingly, half-seriously suggested that they go to Vegas to get married. They thought about it overnight and told her the next day they thought the idea was a good one. So they got up early that morning, and she drove them to Las Vegas to make it official.

I spoke with a man who came to translate for his longtime friend and his friend's companion of eight years, neither of whom spoke English. The friends made the trip together to help the lovers to tie the knot.

Next I met a British couple with two children in tow. The husband-to-be asked me if I had change for a twenty-dollar bill (which I didn't), so I asked him what he needed. A quarter, to make a phone call to a wedding chapel who'd promised to pick them up, he said. I lent him my cell phone and we struck up a conversation. It turns out that the bride and groom had both been married before, and they wanted this wedding to be entirely different from their previous ones. What could be more different than Vegas?

I saw folks enter the court building who looked like they'd been up all night, drinking and playing the slots. A few middle-aged folks who were trying to get it right this time. Two smartly dressed African American couples who were going to go through this rite of passage together. People from all sorts of places, with all sorts of stories, all with some version of the same dream of wedded bliss.

As I talked with people, I noticed one white limousine after another pull up to the curb. I struck up a conversation with the solicitors who populated the busiest corner outside the marriage license bureau. Their jobs were to press advertisements into the palms of couples who were coming for licenses but did not yet have a place to be married. There are scores of wedding chapels in Las Vegas, and couples make their way through a gauntlet of solicitors to get to the marriage license bureau. They must be fairly successful, because the white limousines sent by various wedding chapels appear every minute or so, ready to carry off the next hopeful couple to their nuptials.

Next I headed over to A Little White Wedding Chapel, where one of the limo drivers told me I could get a good lunch at the Cuban restaurant in the Howard Johnson's next door. He was right—the food was great—and I got a glimpse of the motel's own wedding facilities. After lunch, I went to meet the proprietor of A Little White Wedding Chapel, one of the oldest such establishments in the city. Charolette Richards is a trim and fashionable woman in her seventies. The Wedding Queen of the West,[1] Ms. Richards has been a part of Vegas's wedding industry for over fifty years, and she was intent on explaining her high standards for what goes on in her business. Only properly ordained clergy can be part of her staff (no Internet ordinations for her).

"When people get married here I want to make sure I have the right ministers," she told me, ministers "that marry people with sincerity and honesty." Frank Sinatra got married here back in the days when all the couples who came in were well dressed, the women wearing pillbox hats and the men in suits. But Ms. Richards is not impressed by celebrity. "I'm not a person that follows the stars. I follow the One that made the stars," she told me, describing her work in the wedding chapel business as a "calling."

Ms. Richards's establishment offers multiple levels of customer service. Couples may opt to wear their street clothes (including T-shirts labeled "bride" and "groom" that are sold in the lobby) and be led through a simple, brief ceremony. Or they may choose to enjoy a more elaborate event, complete with rental gowns, rental tuxedos, recorded music, and a live Elvis to sing during the ceremony.

The Little White Wedding Chapel property includes five separate chapels, variously sized and decorated to accommodate the needs of couples, whether they come alone or bring family and friends to observe the wedding. The chapel just off the entrance is, indeed, little and white, with a few rows of painted church pews and an electric organ in the back (the space in front is reserved for the presider, the photographer, and Elvis). The other four chapels, variously sized and housed in an adjacent building, are furnished with red velvet Victorian-style settees; cascading folds of gold lamé adorn stands of silk flowers that frame the minister and couple at the front of each room. Between the two buildings is the Tunnel of Love Drive-Thru, which sports a sky-blue ceiling adorned with cherubs and stars and allows couples driving cars or motorcycles to make their vows to one another without exiting their vehicles.[2] A pink Cadillac convertible can be rented for this purpose as well. At the drive-up window inside the tunnel, an officiant leans out to take care of the financial, legal, and marital transactions in a helpful and efficient manner.

Ms. Richards's entire staff is congenial. Among them are the motherly woman who came out from the counter where she was selling accessories to proffer a tissue and instruct a young bride and groom to spit out their gum; the limousine driver poised to take the next call from a couple waiting at the marriage license bureau; Chad, the Elvis impersonator, who waits around during the day until his services are needed, and really does have a pretty good voice; and the eighty-something "adopted mother" of Ms. Richards who plays the organ before, during, and after the services in the diminutive white chapel.

All that attention to detail draws hundreds of people a year. During my visit I met an Irish couple renewing their vows after ten years (the wife cheerily snorted while repeating "for richer or poorer"), a young white couple in faded jeans (the bride rolled her eyes and said "yeah" when I offered my best wishes), and another youngish couple who waited to wave to their children back home in Tennessee while a parent fumbled with a cell phone. Meanwhile, a large Latino family gathered outside on the Astroturf under the gazebo. In the lobby, a fashionable middle-aged French couple waited stiffly on a pew in the lobby until an officiant was free.

Three officiants were on duty the day I visited, as front desk staff sorted the couples who walked through the door, sending them to the next available minister. In the midst of the hubbub of couples presenting their licenses and paying their fees, each officiant was introduced to the couple who was next in line. The officiant asked three questions: (1) Do you have any rings? (2) Is anyone walking the bride down the aisle? and (3) Do you want prayer or not? The couple was then whisked into the chapel best suited for their needs and, in just a few minutes, heard advice about what makes for a good marriage, made their vows to one another, and shared a kiss. After exchanging embraces and words of thanks, they were soon swept from the chapel and out onto the street while another couple took their place.

As unlikely as it might seem, one could argue that Las Vegas can teach the church a thing or two about weddings. First, a Vegas wedding chapel will meet you where you are. Whether you are in a T-shirt and jeans or a fluffy white gown, you are welcome. No judgment, no expectations.

Second, there's no time like the present. No need for two-year engagements while wedding planning takes over the lives of couples and their parents, adding what amounts to a full-time job to the usual stressors of modern life.

Third, and most important, weddings do not have to be expensive. The basic fee at A Little White Wedding Chapel is fifty-five dollars. Couples can choose from packages that will, of course, drive up the price. But it is conceivable that a wedding could cost a couple of hundred dollars instead of tens of thousands of dollars. In an era when the wedding industry drives the decisions that brides and their mothers make, the church could use a reminder that a wedding doesn't "have to" look a certain way.

That is a hard sell, though, to women who have been trained from an early age to imagine themselves as brides. In her illuminating book, *One Perfect Day: The Selling of the American Wedding,* Rebecca Mead points out that the wedding industry is big business, and brides are, first and foremost, consumers. Even those women who promise themselves they are not going to get sucked in to all the hype end up at the CVS counter with twenty-five pounds of bridal magazines.[3]

Reporting a conversation with a group of brides-to-be, Mead describes the range of answers she received to the question "What's a wedding for?" For some, it was about family; for others, a party with friends. Others recognized a religious aspect to the nuptials, while still others, decidedly atheist, saw it as an opportunity for fun. During the discussion, they all searched to define what would make their weddings significant. "But there was no consensus on where that significance lay; indeed, there were contradictions," explains Mead. "A wedding was a celebration of family; it was a celebration of self. It was a religious sacrament; it was an excuse for a party. It was an expression of personal taste; it was an enactment of tradition. What a wedding was for, it seemed, was up for grabs."[4]

These women did share one common experience, however; "each had encountered a wedding industry intent upon ensuring that her experience of being a bride—whatever else it meant to her, culturally and personally—amounted to a transformation into a new kind of consumer."[5]

My own experience as a mother of the groom, which serendipitously coincided with a yearlong sabbatical during which I was conducting research on weddings, confirmed Mead's findings. A visit to the Newport Wedding Show offered a glimpse into the sorts of pressures to which brides are exposed. Bakers offered samples of wedding cakes, cupcakes, cakepops, and cakeballs. Florists outdid one another with extravagant designs for bouquets, arbors, pews, tabletops, corsages, and all varieties of dramatic displays. Photographers showed videos and exhibited elaborate photo books that showed attractive couples posing before breathtaking vistas. Reception venues showcased plated samples of the dinners they would serve, while waitstaff circulated with trays of hors d'oeuvres and champagne. Models descended a dramatic staircase, showing off the season's most exquisite gowns and headpieces. And then there were the vendors that I did not expect to see: those selling LASIK surgery, Botox treatments, spa packages for the female members of the wedding party, and mortgages. Research shows that brides also receive solicitations for home equity loans (to finance the wedding), dance lessons, laser hair removal . . . and the list goes on.

Lest I seem completely joyless, let me hasten to add that I utterly enjoyed the catered meals, top-shelf cocktails, and exquisite flowers that accompanied my own sons' weddings. I was reminded—thankfully—that getting married is an occasion worthy of a great celebration. "I happen to like marriages," one Lutheran pastor in Minnesota told me. "I'm even fond of the ritual excess of weddings. Because of its nature as a life passage, because of its nature as a feast, I think something's right about a little excess for the sake of the day." "Look at John 2," a colleague chimed in, referring to the story of Jesus at the wedding at Cana. "A truckload of wine backed up at the end of the party!"

Some countercultural waves can be seen; couples may decide to have a potluck meal after the nuptials or offer an array of cookies at a simple reception. When my cousin married, several family members and friends gathered flowers from another friend's prolific garden, arrayed them on an arbor, and made the bride's bouquet. A rising number of couples are holding wedding weekends at summer camps, and even the editorial director for *Martha Stewart Weddings* claims to have attended weddings where the guests ate s'mores around campfires.[6] Traditionally, Mexican couples are aided by the whole community when they marry. Friends and family members take responsibility for various aspects of the wedding—some provide the cake, others pay for musicians, still others give favors. Some sing, others provide the dinner or the drinks. Every part of the celebration is touched by someone close to the couple.[7]

In spite of such trends, it remains true that there are tremendous forces at work when any couple are planning their nuptials—whether they are the products of New York society or candidates for the reality show *My Big Fat Gypsy Wedding*. The average cost of a wedding in America is estimated at around thirty thousand dollars, though Manhattanites can expect to pay far more and residents of Utah considerably less.[8] That figure may be misleading; as one journalist has noted, when the median costs are calculated, wedding costs are several thousand dollars less, and most couples are not spending the equivalent of the down payment on a home or the cost of a new car on their nuptials. Nevertheless, it is possible for couples (or their parents) to spend more than they can afford.

The forces of marketing are not directed just at young brides, however. Parents buy Wedding Barbie dolls for their daughters. Little girls board flights from Orlando, Florida, wearing white mouse ears with veils attached. Soap operas and reality shows still make a big deal about weddings. A fifty-billion-dollar wedding industry[9] markets to the dreams of grown-up little girls who pin their favorite ideas for dresses, toe rings, cakes, and koozies on Pinterest and browse the favorites of other soon-to-be brides. They consult wedding-planning Web sites like The Knot with religious fervor, following "the ultimate wedding checklist," ogling "1000+ wedding dress photos," and passing judgment on "500+ gorgeous cakes" as they plan the big event.[10] Online retailers provide "inspiration and guidance" for those planning nuptials. And who hasn't watched at least one episode of *Say Yes to the Dress*?

Many couples are choosing destination wedding packages

as a way to gather far-flung family members and friends, to have a unique experience in an exotic setting over several days, or in an attempt to escape the fuss of planning a wedding on one's own. Hotels and resorts all over the world market to such couples. Perhaps the ultimate fairy-tale wedding venue is Walt Disney World in Orlando, where a couple may be transported to the Wedding Pavilion by Cinderella's Coach ($2,500). Disney's Fairy Tale Weddings & Honeymoons program offers a wide range of possibilities, from a simple ceremony with eighteen guests (with a bouquet, boutonniere, wedding cake, champagne, and one violinist) to "a wedding conducted in Disney's MGM Studios theme park, with the couple and guests cast as movie stars being mobbed by Disney employees enacting the roles of avid movie fans."[11] The crown jewel, however, is the plantation-style pavilion that waits at the end of a gated bridge crossing the Seven Seas Lagoon. Along with the state-of-the-art audio and videography equipment (tastefully concealed, of course), an organ stands ready for a Disney organist to play "Someday My Prince Will Come" from *Snow White* or "When You Wish Upon A Star" from *Pinocchio*.[12] The marketing staff are clear about their goals: if couples have an enchanting Disney World wedding and honeymoon experience, they will be more likely to return for anniversaries, vow renewals, and trips with their future children.

Mead points out that in America, weddings are seen as opportunities for self-expression. At the same time, however, a wedding is an occasion that evokes a strong desire to "observe some form of propriety . . . a desire to enact a role that has been scripted by some source more authoritative than their own powers of invention."[13] In a culture where novelty is highly valued, it is not clear where the source of this authority lies. Mead contends "that the wedding industry has eagerly stepped into this vacuum of authority, and that as a consequence the American wedding is shaped as much by commerce and marketing as it is by those influences couples might prefer to think of as affecting their nuptial choices, such as social propriety, religious observance, or familial expectation. Becoming engaged amounts to a change in one's social status . . . but it also marks the moment of transformation into a potential consumer of bridal products."[14]

SOMETHING MORE?

Mead's assertion that couples are consumers seeking guidance from some authority—any authority—ought to prick up the ears of a church that has lost its way when it comes to weddings. If, in fact, couples are seeking some authority or guidance, why is the church allowing the wedding industry to provide it? If the church is going to continue participating in weddings, we need to provide couples with an alternate vision to the one that drains their bank accounts or those of their parents (or, worse, puts them into debt) and allows the media—or the marketing staff at Walt Disney World—to dictate what a wedding should be like. Perhaps Disney, then, can alert us to couples' unwitting identity as consumers, while Las Vegas might show the church that economy, expediency, and simplicity are possible when it comes to weddings.

It may be what's missing in a Vegas wedding, however, that has the most to teach the church. At the end of a day exploring the Vegas wedding scene, I was left feeling disturbed and demoralized. Gradually, I realized that this came from the lack of three things: a community, a story, and a way of life. As I recalled the events of the day, I was struck with the sense of isolation that pervaded both the marriage license bureau and the wedding chapel: the English couple, clutching the hands of their children, so many miles from their home; the gum-chewing couple looking oh so young and unenthused; the well-dressed French couple who seemed to have expected something very different; and, in the midst of it all, the realization that no couple can succeed at marriage alone. A look at the history of marriage reveals that a couple marrying for love, independent of family concerns and loyalties, is a relatively recent construct. Until the nineteenth century, marriages were arranged or encouraged on the basis of economics; for both farmers and gentry, the joining of families helped to ensure their stability and growth. Indeed, this is still the case in a number of countries around the world. Yet Americans in the early twenty-first century see marriage as a private affair rather than one that takes place within a framework of relationships, often leaving them without family support, social networks, or ties to a religious community.

At its best, the church is able to provide a community within which couples may contemplate, celebrate, and live into marriage. Rather than walking down an aisle to meet a minister who is a stranger in the midst of a room of empty chairs—or idling at the window where a presider leans out to collect a fee and say the necessary words—a couple who marries within a church community is surrounded with people who know them, love them, and support them. In some cases, wedding guests voice their affirmation of the marriage and promise to do everything in their power to uphold it.[15] Those who attend Quaker weddings affix their signatures to the marriage certificate to acknowledge their presence and pledge their ongoing care. In this day and age, of course, those who gather for a wedding often are not all from the local community; friends and family often travel long distances to join together, and destination weddings are popular even among practicing Christians. Nevertheless, a couple with ties to a particular church community may indeed experience the sense of being part of a larger body of people—the body of Christ—who cares what happens to their marriage.

Added to this sense of marriage as a private affair is the lack of a larger narrative within which couples may understand their life together. Although the weddings I observed at A Little

White Wedding Chapel were all conducted by Christian ministers, each presider chose his or her own words without reference
to a larger Christian story. One minister began the service by
saying that marriage is "two people becoming one. It's not one
person dominating the other, neither is it rules or regulations.
But it's the two of you, hand in hand and heart in heart, loving only each other." Toward the end of the service, he counseled the couple before him that by filling their marriage with
love, laughter, and communication, they would enjoy "a long,
prosperous, and blessed marriage." (This was declared just
before Elvis, known to his friends as Chad, started the recorded
accompaniment and launched into singing, "Lord, Almighty,
I feel my temperature rising. . . .") Nothing was spoken that
caused offense, but neither was anything said about this couple
being connected to anyone else. Furthermore, the story of their
marriage was in no way related to the story of the God who
made them, claimed them, and blessed them, or to a body of
believers who would pray for them, listen to them, encourage
them, and support them.

Contrast this scene to how Monica Wood describes the
young priest in her novel *Any Bitter Thing*: "Of all his pastoral
duties, marrying brings him the most pleasure. . . . When he
utters the word 'sacrament,' the engaged couple lift their faces
as one face. The word is a poetic intrusion, crisp with conso-
nants, the very sound of it both precise and evocative. He intro-
duces the word with gravity, a hint of melodrama. Even the
ones who come reluctantly, at the behest of Catholic parents
footing the bill, or out of plain nostalgia for the rituals of their
childhood, even they perk up at this unexpected word for what
they are about to do and promise."[16]

Regardless of how committed the couple is to the church,
this priest allows his own joy in, and marvel of, the mystery of
marriage to spill over, giving a hopeful couple the sense that
the life they are beginning together is connected to something

larger than they are. The question of whether his church, or any church, continues to help couples connect the story of their marriage to the larger story of God and God's people is another matter; but at least, here, there is a glimpse of something more.

A day in Vegas awakens an urge toward a sort of evangelism to share Christian theology and practices, the desire to tell anyone who will listen that their marriage can be a place where Christ is made present, where glimpses of the glory of God can be seen, and where the Holy Spirit upholds, guides, challenges, and sustains. If we will mine them, the riches of the Christian story can offer great gifts to people who would be married, and Christian theology can provide the church with something to say into the near vacuum that has been created by the trends of the time.

Yet the church has been floundering, buffeted by winds of rapid social change and powerful economic forces, with little to say. While ministers are struggling to find their footing, wedding coordinators sweep past them, taking charge of ceremonies, pushing Communion tables and baptismal fonts out of the way. No wonder that Hollywood depicts clergy as paper cutouts at best or, at worst, like Rowan Atkinson nervously calling upon the "Holy Spigot" in *Four Weddings and a Funeral*. We haven't made a very good impression.

STAYING IN THE MARRIAGE BUSINESS

Some argue that the government should get out of the marriage business and leave things to the church. Others argue that the church should get out of the marriage business and let all couples be married by the state. My hunch is that neither of these is likely to happen in the foreseeable future. Individual congregations and their pastors will continue to make decisions about how they will (or will not) be involved in the contracting and blessing of marriages. If the church stays in the wedding business, however, we need to offer couples both a new approach to wedding planning and a deeper understanding of marriage, informed by Christian faith—whether or not it is a faith they share.

Some families have the means to spend a great deal of money on a wedding celebration. Yet so many others do not. A friend and colleague described to me how he approached this issue in his former church, where it was not uncommon to hold fifty weddings a year. Given the number of couples involved, he conducted group premarital counseling sessions. "The first night," he said, "I'd bring a fire pit into the room and bring a whole stack of bride magazines and all kinds of wedding resources that people use, and we would do an exercise. 'What are some of the pieces of advice you've had about the perfect wedding? Write them down.' Then we'd stick them in the fire pit and set them on fire." It allowed them, he said, to begin the conversation in a different way, to consider how the church could help them think about not just the wedding day but also what it means to be partnered in love, now and in the years to come. To stay in the wedding business, the church must have something better to offer than a center aisle or good advice. In short, we must have something worth giving away—to believers and nonbelievers alike.

Baptist minister B. J. Hutto tells the story of a clergy friend named Matthew who is trying to do just that. When a young woman who had grown up in his church came to premarital counseling sessions with her fiancé, he asked them why they wanted to be married in a church. It turned out that the idea was the bride's mother's; the young man was not a believer, and the couple did not mind being married in the family church. Matthew explained that they would have conversations about Christian marriage, the Christian faith, how Christians are "a community shaped by the life, death, and resurrection of Jesus Christ." Offended, the couple left. Soon thereafter, the bride's parents, aunts, and other church members wanted to know why he would "turn down an opportunity to serve a young couple."[17]

In Hutto's view, this pastor was trying to do exactly that—to serve this couple by spending time and energy talking about what it means to be Christian and married. Yet, he writes, "congregations like Matthew's ask anxiously: Why wouldn't a pastor unquestioningly embrace a couple asking to be married? Why would a pastor pass up a chance to draw a young couple into the church? But perhaps," he continues, "that's the wrong question. Perhaps the question we should be asking is, What does it mean for a couple to get married in the church?"[18]

The issue goes beyond personal integrity for pastors or making judgments about who is "Christian enough" to get married in a church. What is at stake is the mission of the church of Jesus Christ, which is to proclaim and enact the good news of the gospel. Are there gray areas? Of course, but for ministers and churches wanting to stay in the wedding business, the gospel is at the heart of the matter.

An unabashedly Christian wedding service reaches beyond the couple being married. One Minnesota pastor told me, "It seems to me that the evangelism piece is not only a part of ministry of pastoral care for the bride and groom but for the two hundred people that show up. . . . There are going to be people who come to that wedding who may or may not want to hear what I say, or may or may not want to hear what the ceremony and the Scriptures have to say about God and this couple. But it's still an opportunity for me to say something about that. It's pretty profound evangelism. I don't get the opportunity to speak to two hundred people who may or may not have a connection with God and the church."

In a letter to the editor of the *Christian Century*, Cherry Neill describes just such an experience. When her son and his bride were married, she wrote, "the presence of the Lord was so heavy that the congregational weeping—and the weeping on the dais—began at the beginning and lasted to the end. . . . The next day an agnostic relative said she'd been up most of the night, tossing and turning, 'trying to figure out the source of all the love in that place.' Of course," said Neill, "the source was the Lord of love."[19]

When Christian faith is at the heart of a wedding—particularly when two believers marry—the love of Christ can, indeed, be palpable. Even when people are nominally Christian, however, or when one is a believer and the other is not, the gospel matters when it comes to marriage. An international Anglican body puts it this way:

> The Gospel message turns the world upside down. This is true when we look at the "world" of marriage, too. In any society, cultural constructions about gender, power and marriage may permit or encourage sexism, exploitation or abuse. By contrast, the life, death and resurrection of Jesus Christ require and, by the Holy Spirit, make possible a Christian construction of marriage that is genuinely life-giving. The marriage of Christians will be marked by Christ-like sacrificial generosity and forgiveness, by radical hospitality and by love that is faithful to the end.[20]

If leading a couple toward a church wedding creates opportunities to share this kind of countercultural message regarding the nature of marriage, then we do, indeed, have good work to do.

At the same time, however, it is important to acknowledge that "Christian marriage" is not a separate category of marriage; better, perhaps, to speak of marriage between Christians. Anyone can enter into marriage; some who do are Christian by virtue of their baptism. As the document written by the International Anglican Liturgical Consultation puts it, "It is as baptized persons, forgiven and reconciled with God through Christ, that Christians come to marriage. The couple bring with them the possibility of having their relationship reflect the intimate, life-giving love that animates and emanates from the community of the Holy Trinity."[21]

This does not mean that only baptized Christians have any hope for a satisfying and generative marriage. It does, however, point to claims about Christian faith and practice that speak into the marriage relationship. Christians are concerned with justice, and Christians who marry profess to one another—and to anyone else with ears to hear—that marriage is just when it is "marked by mutuality, equality, and fruitfulness."[22] Christians care about mercy, too, and practice (at our best) self-giving love and forgiveness. Most of all, Christians are called to proclaim the love of God. One pastor in Minnesota explained it to me this way: "For me at least, it would be to somehow talk about the faithfulness of God through all the things of our life. That's not just for the couple. That's for everyone who is there bringing all sorts of stuff with them. That's at the heart of what makes sense to me . . . to talk about the steadfast love of God."

So, yes, maybe the church should step back from the wedding business but stay wrapped up in the holy work of marriage. To do so, we need to seek clarity about what we are doing, why we are doing it, and how we might do it better. In order to continue on that journey, we turn next to the surprising history of marriage.

Chapter 3

WHAT'S LOVE GOT TO DO WITH IT?

A Short History of Marriage

WHEN FRANK SINATRA SANG THAT LOVE AND MARRIAGE WENT together like a horse and carriage, it was taken for granted that people married for love, that love leads to marriage, and that—at least as far as anyone would admit—lovemaking only happened in the context of marriage. Love and marriage have not always been so closely related, however, as sociologist Stephanie Coontz argues in her book *Marriage, a History: How Love Conquered Marriage.* Not until the eighteenth century did people in Western Europe and North America begin to think of love as the primary reason for marrying or consider that a person should have the freedom to choose his or her own marriage partner. Until that time, marriage was too important to economic survival and too integral to politics to be based on such fickle forces as romantic love and free will.[1] "For most of history," says Coontz, "marriage was not primarily about the individual needs and desires of a man and woman and the children they produced. Marriage had as much to do with getting good in-laws and increasing one's family labor force as it did with finding a lifetime companion and raising a beloved child."[2]

In the ancient world, marriage was the chief way—along with inheritance—of acquiring property. Marriage also produced legitimate heirs.[3] Fathers gave their daughters over to husbands, who thereby assumed control over any assets she brought into the union.[4] In early medieval Europe, rulers used marriage to forge peace treaties and gain land and to establish political alliances.[5] Upper-class families with property brokered marriages between their children to consolidate their resources and accumulate wealth.

From the Middle Ages until the eighteenth century, brides in Europe came with dowries, which were often "the biggest infusion of cash, goods, or land a man would ever acquire." Likewise, "finding a husband was usually the most important investment a woman could make in her economic future."[6] The following account of a marriage between two villagers in late medieval England (which exists because the people being married were children of two prominent citizens) illustrates how the landed gentry marked the marriage:

> On the last day of May 1319, Henry Kroyl senior attended his manorial court at Brigstock, Northamptonshire, and transferred a semi-virgate of land [i.e., several acres] to his son Henry Kroyl junior and his son's intended wife, Agnes, the daughter of Robert Penifader. At the same session, the younger Kroyl endowed his bride with a small house, an adjoining yard, and six rods of land.[7]

No heartfelt vows or affectionate kisses are mentioned here; rather, a real estate transaction joins the lives of these two young folk.

There were, of course, stories and songs of romance, but they were the stuff of fiction in which chivalrous knights wooed beautiful noblewomen (who were usually married to someone else). Love and marriage were considered incompatible. In his treatise *The Art of Courtly Love,* Andreas Cappelanus asserts, "Everybody knows that love can have no place between husband and wife."[8] In twelfth-century France, troubadours and minstrels spread the cult of *fin d'amor,* or courtly love, "a cultural explosion that proclaimed the rights of lovers to live out their passion despite all the objections mustered by society and religion."[9] According to historian Marilyn Yalom, minstrels in French and English courts spun tales of love between "the trio of familiar stock characters: the husband, the wife, and her lover."[10] In Yalom's view, it is not difficult to see how such romantic fantasies would become popular among women of the nobility, who were often wed at a young age to a much older man whose rank or property would bring the family financial or political gain. "Small wonder that she dreamed of an attractive knight her own age with whom she could share transports unknown to conjugal life," asserts Yalom. "If husbands had to put up with stories about wives in adulterous triangles, they could comfort themselves with the hope that such women appeared only in fiction."[11]

Meanwhile, people in the lower classes sought to arrange marriages for whatever economic gain might be possible. Parents married their children to one another so that their fields were adjacent or so that their families were better connected. It took more than one person to manage a farm or a business, and so a mate's practical skills were far more important than his or her good looks.[12] Marriage marked one's entry into "adulthood and respectability" and provided a couple with what we now call "social security, medical care, and unemployment insurance."[13]

People did fall in love, of course. Sometimes, says Coontz, they even fell in love with their own spouses! "At the end of the day—or at least in the middle of the night—marriage is also a face-to-face relationship between individuals."[14] Nevertheless, marriages were not made because people had fallen in love. Such a bond was too important to economic stability and political gain to be based on something as trivial as attraction. Certainly people knew desire and affection, but not necessarily in the context of their marriages.[15] Those who did go against the prevailing norms and married for love did not always have an easy time of it. "He who marries for love," went a saying in early modern Europe, "has good nights and bad days."[16]

In late medieval England, moral treatises exhorted elite urbanites that their marriages should be full of love and cautioned them against arranging unions "for money or other evil causes," which would likely lead to infidelity. Nevertheless, wealthy families usually chose husbands for their daughters. Although young women could sometimes refuse to consent to the match, and some families tried to take into account the happiness of their children, matters of money and politics were paramount.[17] Among rich and poor alike, most expected that it was in the context of marriage that love might grow. This can be seen in the words commonly used to contract a marriage: "May you find it in your heart to have me as your husband," a suitor would ask, intimating that perhaps there would be a chance that genuine devotion might eventually blossom.[18]

By the seventeenth century, Puritan writers saw marriage, in Belden Lane's words, "as a training ground in the learning of affection," and several prominent Puritan couples are known for the joy they took from their married state.[19] One can hear such sentiments in Anne Bradstreet's poem of longing for her absent husband, Simon:

> My head, my heart, mine eyes, my life—nay more,
> My joy, my magazine of earthly store:
> If two be one, as surely thou and I,
> How stayest thou there, whilst I at Ipswich lie?
> . . . .
> Flesh of thy flesh, bone of thy bone,
> I here, thou there, yet both but one.[20]

For Bradstreet and other Puritans, desire for the beloved and the desire for God were all bound up together. And yet who is to say whether young Anne, who was sixteen when she was married to Simon, the twenty-five-year-old assistant to her father, married for love or whether love grew because the two were married.

If they did marry for love, it was not necessarily because they were free to do so. In the American Colonies, parents continued to supervise courtship and approve matches, and going against the wishes of one's parents could have dire consequences. Men were known to back out of a prospective marriage if a woman's parents did not approve, either from fear she would be disinherited or from the specter of unfriendly in-laws. As Coontz puts it, "Few people in the sixteenth and seventeenth centuries believed that 'love conquers all.'"[21]

During the seventeenth and eighteenth centuries, it was thought that people grew to love one another over time after they had been suitably matched. As Coontz says, "People didn't *fall* in love. They *tiptoed* into it." Yet with the dawn of the romantic era, people began to embrace the idea that one could get swept up in passionate feelings and could expect those feelings to be part of a marriage.[22] It wasn't until the late eighteenth century that people began choosing partners because of affection and were actually encouraged to marry because they were in love. Due in large part to the tremendous social and economic changes of the time, "the measure of a successful marriage was no longer how big a financial settlement was involved, how many useful in-laws were acquired, or how many children were produced, but how well a family met the emotional needs of its individual members."[23] Marriage gradually came to be understood as a private contract based on sentiment. Change occurred at different rates in different places, and working-class people did not have the same freedoms as those with means. Little by little, though, across Europe and in the newly formed

United States, people married because they loved each other and valued one another for companionship and comfort.[24]

The nineteenth century brought even more changes, and for the first time marriage was considered central to people's lives. Now people married for "romantic love, intimacy, personal fulfillment, and mutual happiness."[25] Romance did sometimes bloom, on the frontier as well as in the city. Mollie Dorsey lived with her family on their Nebraska homestead. A friend suggested that she set her sights on By Sanford, a young man who had just come to town. They courted for three years, and their love grew steadily. When By finally professed his love for her, Mollie wrote in her journal that she knew he loved her truly and tenderly, and that she could entrust her life to him. "We did not fall madly in love as I had always expected to, but have gradually 'grown into love.' I hope that is an evidence that it will be lasting and eternal."[26] They were married in 1860 and soon set out for their own homestead in Denver. They suffered through a difficult journey, and Mollie was excruciatingly lonely living in the small mining town northwest of Boulder. They lost their first child in infancy. Yet on their second wedding anniversary, Mollie wrote: "Two years married! We spent the afternoon in talking over the old times, bringing up each reminiscence of our lives since we first met. We have passed thro many vicissitudes and had some trials and hardships in our brief married life, but they have only cemented our hearts more closely together. We love and live for each other." Mollie and By enjoyed married life together until his death at age eighty-eight.[27]

For some frontier folks, the old ways persisted. Historian Marilyn Yalom tells of one young man, for instance, who traveled from Switzerland to set up a homestead in Minnesota. A few years later, when he was settled, he wrote to his family back home to ask them to send him a wife. He did not ask for a beauty or a soulmate, but for a strong, capable woman who could care for livestock and keep their log cabin clean and tidy, while he took care of the "man's work." His parents selected a candidate, and the spouses-to-be corresponded for two years. Finally, the young woman traveled the five thousand miles to meet her intended; she arrived in St. Paul on June 4, 1858, and they were married the next day.[28]

For many Americans, however, love had come to be an expected part of marriage by the middle of the nineteenth century. The more people believed that two people could fall in love—and that this was an important, even vital, reason to marry—the more new questions arose. Women wondered if marrying for a reason other than love was immoral; or, to put it another way, was it wrong to marry in order that a mate would provide economic security?[29] Most women were still financially dependent on the support of a husband—or family relations— and had few legal rights, either in or out of marriage.[30]

Other questions surfaced as well. What if a prospective mate did not match up to a woman's expectations? If love waned, could that union be dissolved?[31] How could two people who loved each other live with the usual roles assigned to a husband and wife in marriage, where men were assumed to be in control? So far, the notion of equality between women and men, in either the private or public sphere, was not popular. Husbands were still seen as providers and wives as nurturers, despite the increasing emphasis on intimacy in marriage. Women would, of course, soon gain more independence both economically and politically, but for the time being, the socially sanctioned roles lent stability to marriage.

It is difficult, of course, to generalize about gender roles across class distinctions. Lower-class urban women, whether or not they were married, would work at whatever jobs necessary for economic survival, and women who moved to the western frontier certainly shared in all sorts of labor, even if they did not share equally in authority (though even on the frontier there were distinctions between men's work and women's work).[32]

The difference in marital roles extended beyond household management and into the bedroom. Although Victorian couples may have married because of mutual affection, the "cult of female purity" meant that good wives were not necessarily supposed to be good lovers. "According to the cult of true womanhood," explains Coontz, "only men had sexual desires, but they were supposed to combat their 'carnal' urges." Some men could not think of women they loved and respected in a sexual way. Furthermore, women were often raised to believe that "normal females" lacked sexual desires. Certainly some Victorian husbands and wives enjoyed satisfying sex lives—with one another!—but they do not seem to be the norm.[33] David Shumway, an English professor and student of American culture, points out that for middle-class Victorians, "true love was spiritual, and as a result, it was constant; romantic love was fickle."[34]

Such attitudes soon changed, however, as the sexual reticence of the Victorian era gave way to the rapid social changes of the early twentieth century. Stephanie Coontz calls this transition a move "from sentimental to sexual marriage." A new kind of women's movement emerged as females affirmed the sexual passions of women. Freud's theories became prominent; Margaret Sanger championed birth control and family planning efforts. Young couples went to the movies to watch the actors kiss, then drove to secluded places to practice the techniques.[35] The excesses of the 1920s encouraged greater sexual freedom—along with the expectation for sexual pleasure within marriage.[36]

Not surprisingly, these higher expectations led to rising divorce rates. More and more, people ended their marriages because they failed to be sources of love and intimacy. A century ago, George Bernard Shaw complained that "when two people are under the influence of the most violent, most insane, most delusive, and most transient of passions, they are required to swear that they will remain in that excited, abnormal, and exhausting condition continuously until death do them part."[37] Who could be expected to do that? Yet the social changes that took place in the first part of the twentieth century were not intended to dilute the commitment to marriage. As Coontz explains:

> Deep marital intimacy had been difficult to achieve in the nineteenth century, in the face of separate spheres for men and women, sexual repressiveness, and the strong cultural, practical, and moral limits on a couple's autonomy. Now it seemed attainable. And because the progress of industrialization and democratization had weakened the political and economic constraints forcing people to get and stay married, *such deep intimacy was now seen as the best hope for stability in marriage.*[38]

Perhaps it is not surprising, then, that by the middle of the twentieth century marriage counseling became a thriving profession, as counselors and psychoanalysts came to usurp the role of clergy as the chief advisers on familial relationships.[39]

After the difficulties of the Depression and the Second World War, Americans were ready to return to normal life—and normal life was now considered to include marriage. The United States experienced a golden age of marriage from 1947 through the early 1960s. New homes sprang up, new appliances hit the market, and media encouraged families to have fun and enjoy life. White women tended to stay at home or work at part-time jobs. Those who attended college often dropped out in order to marry. African American women were more likely to work in the marketplace, and fewer were able to attend college. Those who did, however, were less likely than their white counterparts to drop out. Nevertheless, mainstream media depicted the average American family as one where the fathers went to work and the mothers stayed home.

The 1950s model of marriage—a love-based union with a male breadwinner—seemed like it was here to stay. Television portrayed happy, white, middle-class families in shows such as *Leave It to Beaver* and *Father Knows Best*. If the images in the media were to be believed, American suburban families were at the heart of modern society. Of course, marriages were not as idyllic as we were led to believe. And even though race and class differences were real, this TV image of the "typical" American family (which was not typical at all) was heavily marketed and a powerful shaper of popular imagination.[40]

Yet this paradigm, which took a century and a half to become established, unraveled in less than twenty-five years.[41] The catalog of changes that took place over the next decades is too long and too complex to discuss here. The rise of women in the workplace, the invention of the birth control pill, and dissatisfaction of both those who bought into the 1950s model as well as its detractors, combined with a burgeoning civil rights movement, changing laws regarding interracial marriage, and increasing acceptance of divorce, meant that American marriage was in a state of flux.

During the first years of the twenty-first century, marriage continued to undergo great change, as discussed in chapter 1. Still, for many, if not most, Americans, marriage is the most significant commitment they can make. Even as rates of marriage fall and the number of divorces increases, "standards for what constitutes a 'good' marriage have risen steadily." People are less tolerant of lying or keeping secrets in a marriage, and many couples give careful attention to nurturing their relationships and deepening the intimacy between each other.[42]

Clearly this picture is being painted with very broad strokes; one can hardly tell the whole history of marriage in just a few pages. Yet even a brief and generalized account such as this shows what a relatively recent construct a love-based marriage is. It would be naive to insist that contemporary Americans marry only for love, however. While few couples would admit to getting married in order to acquire new cookware, bed linens, or grill utensils, one look at the Pottery Barn wedding registry shows that marriage is still very much about money. When E. J. Graff told people she was writing a book called *What Is Marriage For?* they inevitably quipped that it was for toaster ovens, or silverware, or dental benefits.

> Whether through the kind of dowry that today's middle-class parents pass on in wedding gifts and home down payments, or the corporate mergers of medieval aristocratic families that might have taken years to negotiate, or the small businesses launched when two well-trained vineyarders joined their complementary skills and marriage portions, marriage has always been a key way of organizing a society's economy. Or, to put it more bluntly: marriage is always about money.[43]

One cannot overlook the monetary aspects of marriage, to be sure. Matches are still made between aristocratic families (think John F. Kennedy and Jacqueline Bouvier), and the rich and famous often marry one another (Jay Z and Beyoncé Knowles). Yet love has, for the most part, replaced economic advantage as the central reason for entering such a union. For not much more than a century have people married for love. And it has been even less time since people began to expect from marriage the sort of emotional intimacy, sexual fulfillment, mutuality, and equality that many consider essential for a satisfying life together.

This new paradigm means that we are faced with a new reality that must inform any thinking that the church does about marriage. "The very things that have made marriage as a relationship—and as a love relationship—more rewarding have made marriage as an institution less stable," concludes Coontz. She describes the paradox that is before us:

> Marriage today is fairer, more fulfilling, more intimate, more passionate, more faithful, more loving than most couples of the past would ever dare to imagine. But if it doesn't work out that way, it seems less bearable to people. Relationships that

might have seemed bearable one hundred years ago—even fifty years ago—just seem intolerable as our expectations have risen.[44]

Coontz articulates a key concern that lies at the heart of this inquiry. We cannot go back to a seemingly simpler era—nor would we want to do so. How, then, do we move forward? And what does the church have to say in the face of such a paradox? To begin to answer that question, we must first look at how the church has, and has not, been involved in marriage throughout the centuries.

EARLY CHRISTIAN WRITINGS ON MARRIAGE

The church did not have much to do with marriage for the first thousand years or so of its existence. People contracted their marriages at home, with little or no involvement from the clergy. Marriage was a domestic and legal category, not an ecclesial one.

We know from Scripture, of course, that early Christians got married. Although the New Testament does not have much to say about marriage, we can surmise from the epistles that followers of Christ lived in households much like others of their time. (A fuller exploration of biblical texts regarding marriage follows in chap. 4.) The earliest mention of marriage appears in Paul's letter to the church at Corinth:

> Now concerning the matters about which you wrote: "It is well for a man not to touch a woman." But because of cases of sexual immorality, each man should have his own wife and each woman her own husband. The husband should give to his wife her conjugal rights, and likewise the wife to her husband. For the wife does not have authority over her own body, but the husband does; likewise the husband does not have authority over his own body, but the wife does. Do not deprive one another except perhaps by agreement for a set time, to devote yourselves to prayer, and then come together

again, so that Satan may not tempt you because of your lack of self-control. This I say by way of concession, not of command. I wish that all were as I myself am. But each has a particular gift from God, one having one kind and another a different kind.

To the unmarried and the widows I say that it is well for them to remain unmarried as I am. But if they are not practicing self-control, they should marry. For it is better to marry than to be aflame with passion. (1 Cor. 7:1–9)

If Paul seems less than enthusiastic about marriage, it is, at least in part, because of his conviction that the return of Christ is imminent. He advises his readers to stay in whatever condition they find themselves—married or unmarried—and to serve God as best they can in whatever state.[45] For Paul, celibacy is preferable to marriage because continent people can devote all of their energy to the gospel. Nevertheless, he acknowledges that not all people are given the gift of celibacy and affirms marital sexuality in an ethic of mutual self-giving and esteem. In fact, Paul treats both celibacy and marriage as gifts and does not claim that one state is better than the other, despite the way some in the church would come to interpret this text.[46]

One of the most widely quoted early Christian writers on marriage is the North African theologian Tertullian, who wrote prolifically during the end of the second century and the beginning of the third. In a treatise titled *To His Wife*, he offers an idyllic view of what marriage between Christians can be:

How beautiful, then, the marriage of two Christians, two who are one in hope, one in desire, one in the way of life they follow, one in the religion they practice. They are as brother and sister, both servants of the same Master. Nothing divides them either in flesh or in spirit. They are, in very truth, *two in one flesh*; and where there is one flesh there is also but one spirit. They pray together, they worship together, they fast together; instructing one another, encouraging one another, strengthening one another. Side by side they visit God's

church and partake God's banquet, side by side they face difficulties and persecution, share their consolations. They have no
secrets from one another; they never shun each other's company; they never bring sorrow to each other's hearts. Unem-
barrassed they visit the sick and assist the needy. . . . Psalms
and hymns they sing to one another, striving to see which one
of them will chant more beautifully the praises of their Lord.

Hearing and seeing this Christ rejoices. To such as these
He gives His peace. *Where there are two together,* there also He is
present, and where He is, there evil is not.[47]

Although this excerpt could be construed as something of a
love letter from Tertullian to his spouse, it is actually directed
not only to his own wife but to all Christian women.[48] And, as
rapturous as he sounds about marriage between two Christians,
he is just as adamant that one marriage is more than enough. "I
enjoin you . . . to exercise all the continence in your power and
to renounce marriage after my death," he writes. After assuring
her that there is no marriage in heaven, he says that "on that
day we will not resume any disgraceful pleasures. God does
not promise such frivolous, filthy things to those who are his
own."[49] In his later writings he is even more insistent that there
is no place in the church for remarriage.[50]

Tertullian does go on to say that the union of man and
woman was intended to be "the seedbed of the human race,"
and that nowhere is marriage forbidden.[51] But continence is
better. While his language may sound harsh to contemporary
ears, Tertullian's views, like Paul's, must also be considered
in light of his expectation that the Parousia is imminent. The
coming of Christ requires the church's "total and immediate
sanctification."[52]

For the next three centuries, Christian writers expressed a
wide range of views regarding marriage through their sermons,
letters, and other writings. Some rejected sex (and therefore
marriage) as a sinful result of the fall; some argued that the
Creator intended marriage and procreation as good gifts. For

others, celibacy is upheld along with marriage as a worthy way of serving God—both are forms of ministry.[53]

Once Constantine became emperor of the Roman Empire and Christianity became the religion of the land, the church faced a wide range of views and practices among its new converts. John Chrysostom, presbyter of Antioch and one of the most eloquent and influential preachers of the fourth century, put forth a view of marriage in which two people are drawn together by desire (which is a gift from God) yet live without an attachment to goods or money. While Chrysostom urged monk-like asceticism (if not celibacy) on Christian couples, the Roman monk Jovinian taught that baptism made all equal in God's sight, whether they were virgins, widows, or married. For Jovinian, then, celibacy is not superior to marriage. Although his anti-ascetic views were condemned by the bishops of Rome and Milan, his ideas continued to spread, eventually impelling Augustine to expound upon his own thoughts regarding marriage.[54]

Written in 401 CE, Augustine's *The Good of Marriage* represents the first significant theological work on the topic, and its influence on subsequent generations is enormous.

Augustine, too, considers marriage to be God-given, and for three distinct purposes. First, marriage is for the procreation of children (*proles*). Children are a good (or benefit) of marriage in two ways: they are the "one honorable fruit" of their parents' sexual relationship, and "their very presence in the household tempers the lust of their parents."[55]

Second, marriage affords a "mutual fidelity" (*fides*) by which couples fulfill the conjugal debt to one another and, in doing so, protect one another from fornication. This fidelity is a "natural association" between the sexes that extends beyond their ability to procreate. "In a good marriage," Augustine asserts, "even if it has lasted for many years and even if the youthful ardor between the male and female has faded, the order or charity between husband and wife still thrives. . . . Even if both of their bodies grow weak and almost corpselike, yet the chastity of spirits joined in a proper marriage will endure."[56]

"Compared to the views of many earlier and contemporary Christians," opines historical theologian David G. Hunter, "Augustine's perspectives on marriage appear remarkably well balanced. Lurking beneath the surface, however, was a problem. . . . his belief that the sin of Adam has irrevocably damaged human nature, particularly in its sexual desires."[57] Indeed, Augustine's attitudes regarding sexual intercourse—even in marriage—are troublesome, not only to twenty-first-century hearers, but to some of his contemporaries as well. For Augustine, sexual intercourse for the purpose of procreating "carries no fault." Conjugal relations with a spouse "for the sake of satisfying lust . . . carries a forgiveable fault [*venialis culpa*] because of marital fidelity. Therefore, abstention from all intercourse is better even than marital intercourse that takes place for the sake of procreation."[58] It should be noted that not all fourth-century theologians viewed sexuality as Augustine did; there are those who affirmed the goodness of marriage and procreation.[59] Yet Augustine's voice has been heard most loudly across the centuries.

In spite of Augustine's deep concern about concupiscence, he claimed that "the unifying bond of marriage is so strong that, although it is created for the purpose of procreation, it may not be dissolved for the purpose of procreation." In other words, a marriage that does not produce children is still an indissoluble bond. This bond is so strong, in fact, that he asserts that there is attached to marriage "a kind of sacramental significance [*sacramentum*] . . . something greater than could arise from our feeble mortality." Even when a couple divorces, he argues, the two remain spouses, despite their separation. Non-Christians live under a different ethic, he points out; they may remarry anyone they choose. Christians, however, commit adultery if they remarry after a divorce.[60] This sacramentality is the third good of marriage in Augustine's view. "These things," he writes, "namely offspring, fidelity, and the sacrament, are all good, and because of them marriage is good." Yet he goes on to qualify his pronouncement by saying that "it is certainly better and holier not to set out to have children physically, and to keep oneself free from any activity of that kind, and to be subject spiritually to only one man, Christ."[61]

Augustine was deeply troubled by the existence of sexual desire. And yet he saw marriage as a foretaste of the unity with God that all Christians would one day enjoy. Although he considered celibacy the greater calling, he valued marriage for the bond of friendship it created between husband and wife— one that would "long outlast the relatively short interlude of active sex."[62]

It is important to note that Augustine's use of the term "sacrament" does not reflect later, more precise definitions of the term. Augustine did not consider marriage to be in the same category as baptism or Eucharist, but he did compare marriage to baptism. In the same way that a person cannot undo baptism, neither, argued Augustine, could one dissolve a marriage. Furthermore, although he considered it good for Christians to marry, he did not approve of divorce and remarriage. Remarriage, he reasoned, was invalid because marriage was indissoluble, as is Christ's union with the church (cf. Eph. 5:32). As Philip Reynolds points out, "The arrival of the regime of indissolubility was a great leap forward in the Christianization of marriage. It brought marriage into the Church; it distinguished marriage in the Church from marriage among pagans and among the Jews; it distinguished the Christian law of marriage from Roman law; and it set marriage above merely human standards."[63]

Here at the end of the fourth century and beginning of the fifth, then, is laid the foundation for what will become what Reynolds calls "the normative Western position" regarding divorce and remarriage; what would eventually become established throughout the Western church (but never in the East) was fairly new with Augustine. In time, the church would declare that divorce is allowable only in cases of adultery, and that husbands and wives both have the right to seek the dissolution of a marriage. Even in the case of licit divorce, however, neither spouse may remarry while they are both still alive, for the subsequent marriage would be considered invalid and adulterous.[64]

While a thoroughgoing study of Augustine's theology of marriage goes far beyond the bounds of this work, it must be said that Augustine's views continue to shape contemporary thought. His "three goods" became the basis for traditional Catholic teaching on marriage and, since Protestant theologies emerged in response to that of the medieval church, Augustine's views continued to influence, in one way or another, ecclesial debates and doctrines. Furthermore, the introduction of the idea of marriage as being somehow sacramental—and therefore, *by definition*, indissoluble, led the church to focus on the legalistic meaning of a sacrament rather than the mystery that is a marriage between two people.[65]

MARRIAGE AND THE CHURCH: EARLY RITES

For early Christian writers, marriage was something human beings did; there was no such thing as "Christian marriage," but simply marriage between two people who were Christian (as well as marriage between Christians and nonbelievers). Not until Augustine was there any sense that marriage between Christians was somehow different from marriage among pagans, Jews, or Roman citizens. Neither Paul nor any other biblical writer discusses *how* Christians are to get married, and though a few early documents indicate that there may have been some sort of ritual involving the church, in the early centuries of the church Christians got married the way everyone else did.[66] Marriage was primarily a family matter, and rituals varied from community to community, though some patterns can be noted. Among those in the lower classes, a couple could be considered married when they began living together. For others, there may have been some sort of domestic betrothal rite, a handing over of the bride, and a celebration of the consummation of the marriage.

Sometimes Christians eschewed customs they considered inconsistent with their faith (e.g., "pagan" practices). In other cases, they recognized marriages that the state did not. The Roman church, for example, acknowledged marriages between free women and men who were slaves, even when they did not seek to be married legally. Such couples did not always marry according to Roman law, since the woman and any children of the marriage would be forced to assume the lower status of the husband. Yet the church would bless their unions and consider them married in the eyes of God.[67] On occasion a priest, as leader of the faith community, would be invited to give a blessing to the newly married couple. For a number of centuries, however, having clergy bless a marriage was akin to requesting a house blessing today—it was something that particularly devout people might do, but certainly not the usual practice, and even then, it was usually done only when the groom was himself clergy. Beginning in the late fourth century, clergy who married sought the blessing of the bishop rather than take part in the bawdy procession to the groom's house that was part of many domestic marriage celebrations.[68]

The earliest wedding liturgy in the Western church is thought to date from sixth-century Verona. It is not a complete wedding service; there are no betrothal rites and no vows are spoken. What does appear in the Veronese Sacramentary (also called the Leonine because it was originally attributed to Leo the Great) is a celebration of the Eucharist that likely took place after the marriage was contracted at home, followed by a blessing of the

bride. After giving thanks to God for creating the world, giving
life to all creatures, commissioning human beings to multiply,
and giving Adam a companion, the cleric prays:

> Thus your command to share the marriage bed,
> to increase and multiply in marriage,
> has linked the whole world together
> and established ties among the whole human race.
> This you saw, O Lord, to be pleasing, even necessary:
> that she who would be much weaker than man—
> she being made in his image,
> and he being made in yours—
> once joined to the stronger sex,
> they who were previously two become one;
> while from that oneness of love both sexes derive.

The prayer continues by asking that the woman exhibit the
qualities of biblical brides—that she be "loving to her husband,
like Rachel; wise, like Rebecca; long-lived and faithful, like
Sarah"—and that she be "loyal to one bed . . . serious and mod-
est . . . fruitful with children" until the last day.[69] Apart from the
references to Old Testament matriarchs, the most obvious biblical reference is to the command to "be fruitful and multiply."
In addition to prayers for the bride's fertility is this supplication:
"May she remember that she is called not so much to the lawful pleasures of marriage as to the safeguarding of her promise of fidelity."[70] There is no sense of the church dispensing a
sacrament or pronouncing the indissolubility of the marriage,
although the priest prays that God will "keep in lasting peace
those whom you will join in lawful union [*societas*]." It is not
at all clear whether many people actually went to church for a
nuptial Eucharist.

The marriage liturgy found in the Gregorian Sacramentary—
dating from the eighth century but reflecting the sixth-century
liturgy of Gregory the Great—carries a more official status than
the local Veronese rite but echoes many of the same themes:

the God-given nature of marriage, the weakness of women, the virtues of a Christian wife, and marriage as a companionable estate. The newly composed preface of the eucharistic prayer adds a lyrical note to the text:

> It is truly right and just,
> fitting and for our salvation.
> For you have joined people in marriage
> with the sweet yoke of concord
> and the unbreakable bond of peace.[71]

Much of the nuptial blessing is taken from the Veronese liturgy, although a significant new feature appears: the couple, entering the God-given estate of marriage, inherits the covenant established at creation and prefigures the marriage between Christ and the church (i.e., the marriage of the Lamb in Revelation 21):

> O God,
> you made all things out of nothing by your power.
> When you had laid the foundations of the universe,
> you created man in the image of God,
> and made woman as man's inseparable helper,
> bringing the woman's body into being
> out of the man's flesh,
> teaching us thereby
> that what it had pleased to create
> out of an original unity
> must never be put asunder.
> O God,
> you have consecrated the bond of marriage
> with such an excellent mystery
> as to prefigure in the covenant of marriage
> the sacrament of Christ and his Church.[72]

In marrying, the couple takes on "a larger, archetypal identity, in which both past and future meet"; their experience echoes that of God and Israel and anticipates the eternal union of Christ and the church.[73]

CHURCH WEDDINGS

Meanwhile, in Spain, a rich marriage liturgy evolved over several hundred years. By the eleventh century, two chief liturgical collections, *Liber ordinum* and *Liber antiphonarius*, provide texts for betrothal that include the giving of a ring. Also included is a blessing of the bedchamber, which would have taken place on the Saturday before the Sunday nuptial mass. This rite includes a local custom of sprinkling salt (perhaps as an exorcism; this was sometimes a part of ancient baptismal liturgies) and praying for the virtue of the couple:

> May the words and actions of those who enter here
> to celebrate their marriage be so proper
> that they are never swept away by desire
> to the shipwreck of passion.[74]

Centuries after Augustine, the church is still clear that marriage is about sex for the purpose of procreation and not romantic love or passionate lovemaking.

After the preliminary rituals, a full Eucharist is celebrated. Then the couple to be married approach the priest. The parents of the woman ("girl" in the text) hand her over to the priest, who then "veils the couple with a pall or sheet, placing on top of it a cord of white and purple."[75] The priest speaks a nuptial blessing, praying for fidelity, the gift of children, and the ability to "render to one another the debt of marriage in such a way as never to cause offense to you." He asks God to "grant to this your maidservant, N., whom we have just joined in the bond of matrimony, genuine resources of gracious sweetness and true love for the husband she is marrying." As the Roman church exerted more power over the church, the Spanish liturgy was suppressed after the eleventh century, but this example shows the incorporation of local customs into the liturgical life of the people.

The most significant changes in medieval marriage rites emerged in the eleventh and twelfth centuries in England and France, where church weddings were more common.[76] Here we begin to see elements that still appear in contemporary weddings—the couple speaking vows to one another, the giving of rings as part of the marriage service (as opposed to the betrothal), and a kiss. An English rite from the era (from the Bury St. Edmunds missal) shows the betrothal rite—where the couple is asked whether they consent to the marriage—being held at the church door. After prayers are offered, and both the bride and groom have given their consent, a ring is given to the bride, and the bridegroom says:

> With this ring I thee wed,
> this gold and silver I thee give,
> with my body I thee worship,
> and with this dowry I thee endow.[77]

After receiving the ring, the coins, and the dowry, the bride "falls to the feet of her husband"! She rises, the priests offers several more prayers, then he leads the couple into the church as they carry lighted candles. More prayers commence at the altar, including the supplication that God "sanctify your hearts and join you together in the companionship and affection of genuine love."[78] Subsequent prayers ask God for spiritual blessing, health, peace, and the grace to be obedient to God, serving God together until the last day. After the mass, the bridegroom receives a kiss of peace from the priest, and then he kisses the bride. Once the couple arrives home, blessings are said over the couple, a cup, and their bedchamber, that the couple may be prosperous and enjoy a long life together.[79]

Although it may not seem extraordinary to contemporary ears, the giving of consent to the marriage in the vernacular was significant. Previously, betrothal happened informally, sometimes with a ring. From the twelfth century on, however, those who seek the church's blessing on their marriage must stand at the church door and say out loud, in their own language, that they desire to be married.[80] This is such an important concept that Peter Lombard explains it thus: "It is the bond which is established by the words of consent—when they say 'I take you for my husband . . . I take you for my wife'—which makes the marriage." It makes a difference, he says, that this is expressed verbally and in the present tense (i.e., not as a future promise). Even if they do not "mean [it] in their hearts, still the force of those words of consent—'I take you for my husband' and 'I take you for my wife'—is such as to constitute a marriage."[81] Even when parents arranged marriages for their children, the church insisted that those being married voice their own consent. Other medieval theologians commented on the importance of mutual consent as well, while continuing to echo the foundation Augustine established.

MARRIAGE AS SACRAMENT

Meanwhile, parents were still arranging marriages for their children, especially those from political or aristocratic families. By the time of the Fourth Lateran Council (1215), the church urged couples to marry with their parents' consent, in the presence of witnesses, and after undergoing counseling with a priest. Throughout the twelfth and thirteenth centuries, theologians debated when marriage became a sacrament and how it did so. For some, the consummation of the marriage was the key; others argued that the carnal act of intercourse—which could so easily become sinful even in marriage—could hardly be considered a means of grace. Still others, including John Duns Scotus, suggested that the nuptial blessing said by the priest at the wedding made the marriage a sacrament, a view which had some appeal, since that act could be considered parallel to the sprinkling of water in baptism or the giving of bread and wine in the Eucharist. Yet this did not account for marriages that were made without involvement of a priest, and to designate those marriages "unsacramental" was akin to severing the couple from the church. It had become the consensus view by the late thirteenth century that the exchange of vows made the marriage a sacrament, whether or not those vows were spoken in the context of a church wedding, and whether or not the marriage was consummated. As John Witte explains it, "It was the mutual exchange of wills, the genuine union of mind to be married, that triggered the conferral of sacramental grace."[82]

Thomas Aquinas offered an argument for the sacramental nature of marriage that would prove to be the foundation upon which future Catholic doctrine would be built. He explained that marriage is a natural estate, because marriage is for the purpose of nurturing children. Marriage is also contractual, however, because a couple makes an agreement to stay together for the sake of their own good, the good of their children, and the community at large. Finally, Thomas argued, marriage is sacramental because it is a spiritual reality that not only legitimizes sexual intercourse and gives greater significance to the procreation and nurture of children, but also becomes an instrument of grace. Marriage is more than a contract; it is a lasting union of the same sort of fidelity, love, and sacrifice that could be seen in the union of Christ and the church.[83]

One can hear the echoes of Augustine's own formulations in those of Thomas Aquinas. Yet Thomas goes further, claiming that marriage is named a sacrament to "demonstrate its spiritual efficacy." Where Augustine concluded that marriage should not be dissolved because it is a symbol of Christ's union with the church, now marriage could not be dissolved since it was defined as an enduring conduit of sacramental grace.[84]

Naming marriage as a sacrament reflects the recognition of this intimate union as a significant relationship that is a way of living one's life in the church. It also brought marriage under the purview and power of the church and reflected the newly emerging pastoral identity of clergy. Most important, marriage is now seen as an event, a ritual celebration like baptism, and not only as an estate. Scholars would continue to debate the meaning of marriage as both an event and an estate, but the groundwork was laid.[85] The theologians of the era synthesized a thousand years of thought on the matter and shaped the understanding of marriage in the Catholic Church, one that would be canonized at the Council of Trent (1563).

A fourteenth-century marriage rite from a Cistercian abbey in central France is the first complete known text of a wedding service, providing liturgy for the betrothal, the marriage service itself, and the blessing of the wedding chamber. Here, the betrothal occurs several weeks prior to the wedding. The couple comes to the church door, and a public announcement of the upcoming marriage (called "the banns") is made for the final time. The bride and groom give their consent to the marriage and exchange vows to take one another as a spouse within forty days.

When the couple return for the wedding, they meet the priest at the door of the church and affirm that they want to be married. Then the bridegroom repeats after the priest the following vow:

> N., I take you to be my wife and my spouse
> and I pledge to you the faith of my body,
> that I will be faithful to you and loyal
> with my body and my goods
> and that I will keep you in sickness and in health
> and in whatever condition it will please the Lord to place you,
> and that I shall not exchange you
> for better or worse
> until the end.

The bride repeats the same vow to the bridegroom. After a blessing of the ring, it is given to the bride, along with a gift of silver, and the groom repeats a ring vow. The silver goes into the bride's purse, not to her family, as had been done in the past. The priest then takes the bride and groom by the hands and leads them into the church, where mass is celebrated. Afterward, blessings over bread and wine, as well as the bedchamber, take place at the couple's home.[86]

The wedding service from the Sarum Manual, which was widely used throughout England in the first half of the sixteenth century, is perhaps the most influential pre-Reformation marriage rite. Here the betrothal and marriage rites are merged; instead of a separate betrothal rite, the couple is now asked to first give their consent and then take marriage vows. The service begins at the church doors, where the priest reads the banns and then, assuming there are no objections to the union, asks the man:

> N., wilt thou have this woman to thy wife
> and love her and worship her and keep her
> in sickness and in health,
> and in all other degrees
> be to her as a husband should be to his wife,
> and all other forsake for her,
> and hold thee only to her to thy life's end.

The bridegroom responds, "I will," then the priest asks the bride:

> N., wilt thou have this man to thy husband,
> and be buxom [obedient, compliant] to him,
> love him, obey to him, and worship him,
> serve him and keep him in sickness and in health,
> and in all other degrees
> be unto him as a wife should be to her husband,
> and all other to forsake for him,
> and hold thee only to him to thy life's end.

The bride replies, "I will," then either her father or a friend gives her hand to the groom. They then exchange vows that will echo through the centuries:

I, N., take thee, N.,
to my wedded wife,
to have and to hold
(from this day forward),
for better for worse,
for richer for poorer,
in sickness and in health
till death us depart
(if holy Church will ordain),
and thereto I plight thee my troth.

The bride's vow is nearly the same, with one significant addition. After pledging to care for her groom "in sickness and in health," she promises "to be bonoure and buxum [agreeable and compliant] in bed and at board." Both spouses, then, pledge to love and worship (that is, ascribe worth to) and keep one another, yet only the bride promises obedience and compliance in all matters, particularly the most intimate.[87] Afterward, the ring is blessed and the groom gives it to his bride, using words similar to those used in earlier English rites ("With this ring I thee wed . . ."). A series of prayers follows, after which the priest leads the bride and groom to the altar. They prostrate themselves, and the priest invites the gathered congregation to pray for the couple. After the prayers, they move to the south side of the church and a mass commences. Following the Sanctus, the couple lies prostrate at the altar steps again, and a veil is spread over them, held by four clerics. After continuing the prayers and breaking the host, the priest kneels under the veil and speaks additional prayers over the couple. Returning to the altar, the priest continues the prayers of the mass, the veil is lifted, and the couple rises. The priest shares a kiss of peace with the groom, who in turn shares it with his wife, while one of the clerics receives the kiss from the priest and shares it with the rest of the congregation. The mass ends, and the couple go to their home for a wedding banquet; the next night the priest goes to the couple's home to bless their marriage bed (while they are in it!).[88]

The rite just described was printed in 1543 (the first was printed in 1508), not long before Thomas Cranmer issued the first Book of Common Prayer. The Sarum Manual reflected the most recent developments in the marriage liturgy—speaking the consent aloud in front of the priest and making their own vows—and much of this rite would reappear in the Book of Common Prayer, thereby setting the stage for even wider usage. Cranmer would add the words "to love and to cherish" to those vows, which would eventually become "part of the classical international English culture."[89]

MARRIAGE AND THE PROTESTANT REFORMERS

While the English churches were marrying people using the Sarum liturgy, theological and liturgical foment was brewing on the Continent. Protestant Reformers affirmed the naturalist view of marriage as a union that is for the procreation of children and protection from sexual sin. They also considered marriage a voluntary contract established by the mutual consent of both parties. The Reformers, however, denied that marriage is a sacrament.[90] It is, they countered, an "independent social institution" that does not require faith. Nor, they insisted, does marriage confer sanctifying grace. Furthermore, the Reformers denied that celibacy is better than marriage, noting the clergy's aptitude for fornication and concubinage, and rejected the idea that marriage is indissoluble while affirming its goods. Three distinct Protestant traditions emerged around marriage—the Lutheran, the Calvinist, and the Anglican—and the marriage liturgies of each tradition reflect their theological differences.

Martin Luther believed that marriage is instituted and blessed

by God at creation yet maintained that it is a secular association and not a sacrament instituted by Jesus Christ. In Luther's
view, the Catholic Church's understanding of marriage as sacrament was based on a misinterpretation of Ephesians 5:32—
the result of Jerome's translating the Greek *mystērion* (mystery)
into the Latin *sacramentum* a thousand years earlier. The Vul-
gate became the standard Latin translation of the Bible, and
the use of *sacramentum*, Luther insisted, threw the church off
course. In Ephesians, he argued, Paul describes the relationship
of husband and wife as a reflection of that between Christ and
the church but does not intend to say that marriage is a sacrament that confers grace.[91]

Luther himself was a happily married pastor who often said
that his wife, Katarina (whom he nicknamed Mr. Kathy), was
his superior, claiming, "I am Aaron, she is my Moses." He considered marital love the highest sort of love and counseled couples to care for one another spiritually, emotionally, and sexually
and to share in household chores and child rearing.[92] Although
he denied that marriage was a sacrament, he believed that if a
couple asks for the church's blessing, the church should give it.
It should also pray for couples, as well as tell youth about the
importance of marriage. As a result, Luther wrote a three-part
wedding rite that began with publishing the banns. The minister
would announce from the pulpit the couple's intent to marry
and their desire for prayer on their behalf, then instruct anyone
with "anything to say against it" to "speak in time or afterward
hold his peace."[93]

When the day of the marriage arrived, the minister met the
couple at the church door, where he asked each of them if they
desired to marry the other. After saying yes, they exchanged
wedding rings and joined hands. Saying "What God hath joined
together, let no man put asunder," the minister pronounced the
two "joined in marriage" in the name of the Trinity.

Moving into the church to the altar, the minister read the

second chapter of Genesis to the bride and groom and preached a sermon in which he exhorted them to "hear first of all God's commandment concerning this estate." Luther's exhortation began with a reading of Ephesians 5:25–29 ("Husbands, love your wives . . ."), followed by a reading of verses 22–24 ("Wives, be subject to your husbands . . ."), reversing the order that is found in the epistle. The minister continued by describing "the cross which God has placed upon this estate," reading Genesis 3:16–19, in which God names the sorrows incurred by the first human couple as a result of their disobedience. After describing the woman's pain in childbirth and how difficult it will be for the man to provide bread, the minister moved to his third point: "This is your comfort, that you may know and believe that your estate is pleasing to God and blessed by him." In short, Luther instructs the couple on their responsibilities to one another, reminds them that their marriage will be difficult, then reassures them that their union is, nevertheless, blessed. A benedictory prayer concluded the service.[94]

The Lutheran tradition that emerged is a "social model" of marriage—that is, "a social estate of the earthly kingdom of creation, not a sacred estate of the heavenly kingdom of redemption." Marriage is to be governed primarily by the state, not the church, and people are to be encouraged to marry unless they possess the gift of celibacy.[95] Pastors are expected to minister to families, but all people in the priesthood of believers are to counsel those who are contemplating marriage and to admonish those who are thinking about divorce. But the church has no legal jurisdiction over the making or dissolving of marriages.[96]

Calvin's Geneva proved to be remarkably significant in the development of the theology of marriage and its laws. As John Witte Jr. puts it, "If Wittenberg was the Bethlehem of Protestant marriage law, Geneva was the Nazareth." An independent city that declared its affinity with the Protestant movement in 1536, its unique blend of civil and church life enabled rich legal and theological understandings regarding marriage to emerge— ones that would prove influential for centuries to come.[97] John Calvin would take the lead in reforming marriage and family life in Geneva on both the theological and legal fronts.

Like Luther, Calvin saw marriage as an earthly estate, not a sacrament. In his 1536 *Institutes* he called the bond "a good and holy ordinance of God just like farming, building, cobbling, and barbering"[98] that is for mutual love and support, procreation and nurture of children, and protection from sexual sin. Although for Calvin marriage symbolizes the union between Christ and the church, marriage does not confer grace, as the sacraments do.

As Calvin's thinking matured over the years, he developed an understanding of marriage based in the biblical notion of covenant. His theology of marriage was not systematic or consistent—his thoughts must be culled from sermons, letters, commentaries, and legal notes—but his impact was profound. Drawing on the Old Testament prophets, Calvin argues that God draws two people into a covenant relationship with one another just as God draws the believer into a covenant relationship. He argues, therefore, that "God is the founder of marriage. . . . The Scripture says that it is a holy covenant, and therefore calls it divine."[99]

When two people marry, they form a covenant that involves more than the couple. For Calvin and his followers, marriage was "a covenantal association of the entire community." In other words, it took a village to get married in Calvin's day! A couple confirmed their engagement promises and their marriage vows before God, enacting the idea that marriage is a three-party agreement. The couple's parents—who had been entrusted with the nurture of their children—gave their consent. Two witnesses were required to be present, as priests to their peers. The minister's role was to bless the couple and instruct them in the spiritual duties of marriage. Finally, the magistrate registered the marriage, ensuring that they, and their property, were protected. Each party was considered essential to the marriage covenant.[100] Furthermore, a marriage could not be validated without a wedding, for the public event confirmed not only the couple's desires but also the consent of both church and state.[101] Calvin's understanding of marriage as covenant, then, helped to establish a pattern that would become normative in the West—a public act involving the consent of the couple as well as that of their parents, the presence of two witnesses, the blessing of the church, and legal registration—a spiritual and legal reality with clearly articulated, separate roles for church and state.[102]

Calvin subscribed to the traditional goods of marriage—mutual love, procreation and nurture of children, and protection from sexual sin—but he articulated the benefits far differently than Augustine had. Although he cautioned against choosing a mate too quickly or indiscriminately, and urged couples not to marry because of lust, Calvin had a great appreciation for human sexuality. He approved of admiring the attractiveness of a mate and even praised "beauty," "comeliness," "handsomeness," and "elegance of form," usually in women but occasionally also in men. There was nothing wrong, Calvin thought, with gazing at a good-looking person, because attraction served to beget the "secret kind of affection [that] produces mutual love."[103] In marriage, Calvin insisted that couples maintain a healthy sexual relationship even if they advanced beyond the age of childbearing. Marriage sanctifies sex, he believed, and sex is part of a good marriage. Furthermore, if couples did not bear children, Calvin did not consider it grounds for divorce; procreation was just one of the purposes of marriage. Finally, if one spouse became unable to sustain the sexual relationship, the other was to treat him or her with understanding and care, rather than take another sexual partner or seek a separation or divorce.[104]

In Calvin's Geneva, weddings could happen any day that the church gathered—on a Sunday, or on a Wednesday for Bible study—except when Communion was to be celebrated and on certain holy days. The point was that marriage services were to be held in the presence of the worshiping community. Local statutes required virgins to be veiled during weddings and first-time brides to wear wreaths of flowers, unless it was discovered they had premarital intercourse. A picture of a typical Genevan wedding comes from a 1556 travelogue, *The Parisian Passwind*, that gives a vivid description of liturgical life in the city, with a bit of humor thrown in. The narrator describes seeing a groom and his party carrying flowers and retrieving the bride from her home. She is wearing a wedding gown; her hair is flowing loose and her head is veiled (if she is a virgin) and wreathed in flowers (whether she is a virgin or a widow). The bride is accompanied by bridesmaids, who carry bouquets. The groomsmen head up a procession, followed by the couple—"the groom leading his bride by the hand for fear of losing her"—and then the brides-maids, and lead the party to the church door, where "they all take their places and wait for the preacher to start." The author continues, with tongue only partially in cheek:

> After the sermon, the groom takes the bride by her hand again and they proceed to the door of the choir or the steps where the high altar used to be, and there the deacon or the minister in his absence joins them by a ceremony as long or longer than ours, his head uncovered and facing the people, emphasizing that he only does so to ratify in the presence of the church the promise they had already [made] among themselves. Then they all return to the groom's house in the same order, and after dinner everyone retires so that the married couple can chat about their private matters.[105]

Although the author—believed to be a French Franciscan

who spent several months in Lausanne taking note of Reformed life—writes a book that is partly fiction, and even a little risqué, he supplies what scholars believe are vivid and accurate accounts of Geneva's liturgical life.[106]

The Parisian Passwind may have described a Reformed wedding in a breezy style, but Calvin's wedding liturgy—which was based on the work of Guillaume Farel and other Reformers— had a decidedly didactic tone. In *The Manner of Celebrating Holy Matrimony* (1545), Calvin provides ample instruction for the presider and a good deal of biblical exhortation for the couple. The minister, says Calvin, is to tell a husband and wife how they should treat one another, based on Scripture readings from Genesis 2, Matthew 19, 1 Corinthians 7, Colossians 3, 1 Timothy, Titus, and 1 Peter 3. "It would not be irrelevant or useless," he advises, "for the minister to assemble the exhortations and consolations found in these places dealing with this subject and matter," and the liturgy includes the text of a sermon by Calvin.[107] After this biblical exhortation, the minister then asks both bride and groom to consent to the marriage and instructs the congregation to remember the act. It is important to Calvin that both bride and groom consent to the marriage, and that they are doing so honestly and with a sense of the gravity of the union.

The minister then asks the congregation for their own consent and whether anyone knows any impediment to the marriage. After hearing no objection to the union, the pastor then speaks vows: "Do you, N., confess here before God and his holy congregation that you have taken and take for your wife and spouse N. here present, whom you promise to protect, loving and maintaining her faithfully, as is the duty of a true and faithful husband to his wife, living piously with her, keeping faith and loyalty to her in all things, according to the holy Word of God and his holy Gospel?"

The groom simply replies, "Yes." The pastor then asks a

similar question of the bride, who promises to "obey, serving and being subject to him," in addition to remaining faithful and loyal.

Again, the reply is a simple "Yes." The rite proceeds toward its end with the pastor reminding the couple of Jesus' words from the Gospel of Matthew, urging that what "God hath joined together, let no man put asunder," followed by a prayer and words of blessing.[108]

After the usual sermon, the couple spoke vows that reiterated their duties as husband and wife; the final prayer echoed the same. Ritual acts were few, and since weddings were not scheduled on Sundays when Communion was served, there was no Eucharist. Neither were there symbolic gestures familiar to other wedding liturgies of the time—the couple did not kneel at the altar, hold hands, or exchange rings; there was no lifting of the veil or kissing of the bride, and no music of any kind. The service was to be orderly and reverent, so that the couple could hear the Word being proclaimed that day.[109]

Calvin—who presided at more than 275 weddings while at Geneva, most of them in the 1550s—was less concerned with the details of the liturgy than with the fact that couples were married in the midst of the community. He recognized that liturgical diversity was present in the churches and did not consider that to be problematic; what was important was that weddings took place in the church.[110] Since the banns were read for three Sundays before the wedding, many people heard what amounted to an invitation for everyone to attend the wedding, which took place in the church during the usual worship service. As Calvin described it, the minister's responsibility was "to approve and confirm this marriage before the whole assembly." For Calvin, weddings were public events involving the whole congregation.[111] The family and friends of the couple must express their approval, and the Word of God must be proclaimed as husband and wife bind themselves in a sacred union.

Calvin's Marriage Ordinance of 1546 laid out his expectations for how married couples of Geneva would comport themselves. If they fought, they would be reprimanded by the consistory and instructed to leave peaceably with one another. Spousal abuse was strictly prohibited. Yet even in the most troubled marriages, the ordinance did not provide for "separation from bed and board," which had traditionally served as a form of relief without divorce. "An ethic of perpetual reconciliation of husband and wife coursed through the ordinance," and members of the whole community, along with ministers and magistrates, were responsible for encouraging such behavior. Under the most extreme circumstances—such as an incurable disease, impotence, adultery, or desertion—divorce could be arranged, but the process of doing so was lengthy and unwieldy.[112] Engagements could be broken, but marriages could not.

With his covenantal model of marriage, Calvin affirmed the earthly goodness of nuptial union while acknowledging the sacredness of it. He confirmed the idea that a marriage is constituted by mutual consent of two people yet also went beyond the idea of a contract to assert that God is part of the covenant that is made in marriage. In so doing, he added a religious aspect to Luther's social one. "The effect of this," explains Witte, "was to add a spiritual dimension to marriage life in the earthly kingdom, a marital obligation to spiritual life in the heavenly kingdom, and complementary marital roles for both church and state in the governance of both kingdoms."[113] As such, Calvin created a model that would spread throughout the Continent, America, and South Africa and continue to influence Protestant understandings of marriage until the present day.

It is difficult to overstate the significance of the Anglican contribution to the marriage liturgy. The Book of Common Prayer, produced by the well-informed genius of Thomas Cranmer, continues to influence the language of wedding services in the English-speaking world. Although it grew out of a long liturgical tradition—and was informed as well by early Reformation liturgies—England's marriage liturgy sprouted from the soil of ecclesial and political intrigue.[114] In 1503, at the age of twelve, the future Henry VIII, heir to the English throne, was engaged to his brother's widow, Catherine. After debates over canon law and the propriety of the match, Pope Julius II gave a dispensation to Catherine so that she could marry Prince Henry. They did so in 1509, just after he ascended to the throne. After a decade of marriage, Catherine had given birth to six children; all but one, their daughter Mary, were either stillborn or died as infants. Somewhere along the line—because of attraction, desire for a male heir, lack of interest in his wife, or some combination thereof—Henry took a mistress (also named Mary), who bore him a son. (This child would never be considered a legitimate heir to the throne.) Henry began consulting with legal advisers and launched a long and involved series of hearings aimed at having the marriage annulled.

The plot thickened as Henry took another mistress, Mary's sister Anne Boleyn. Meanwhile Catherine began her own legal proceedings in an attempt to stop Henry's quest to end their marriage. Before it was all over, hearings had been held in both Rome and England; legal arguments involved two popes and a good number of canon lawyers; and Lord Chancellor Thomas More and Bishop Fisher were executed for trying to stand in Henry's way. After a seven-year ordeal, the papal court decided that Henry and Catherine's marriage was valid and in accordance with canon law.

Henry, however, had already secretly married Anne Boleyn the previous year. He had also appointed Thomas Cranmer archbishop of Canterbury, and within two months Cranmer proclaimed Henry and Catherine's marriage annulled and validated Henry's union with Anne, in spite of the fact that the two acts required opposing theological and legal arguments. The next year, in 1534, Parliament issued the Act of Succession, which confirmed Cranmer's judgment and affirmed Henry and Anne's daughter, Elizabeth, as heir to the throne. Soon thereafter the Supremacy Act of 1534 became law, and Henry became the self-declared head of the Church of England.

It is hard to miss the irony that a wedding service that would become so influential for centuries to come was crafted against a backdrop of such intrigue! Cranmer shaped the marriage rite in the Book of Common Prayer using the old Sarum rite as its basis, borrowing from other medieval sources and, occasionally, Luther. The first edition appeared in 1549; Martin Bucer did a thorough review, and his critique contributed to the 1552 revision. Another edition was released in 1559 when Elizabeth assumed the crown, but it is identical to the 1552 rite. Only slight changes were made in 1662.

Cranmer moves the wedding into the church, where the couple gathers with family, friends, and neighbors. It is understood that banns have been read on three previous Sundays or holy days. The rite begins with the familiar "Dearly beloved," and the priest explains why the people are there:

> Dearly beloved friends,
> we are gathered together here in the sight of God,
> and in the face of his congregation,
> to join together this man and this woman
> in holy matrimony,
> which is an honorable estate,
> instituted of God in Paradise,
> in the time of man's innocence,
> signifying unto us the mystical union
> that is betwixt Christ and his Church:
> which holy state Christ adorned and beautified
> with his presence and first miracle
> that he wrought in Cana of Galilee,
> and is commended of Saint Paul
> to be honorable among all men.[115]

The opening statement continues by affirming that marriage is not entered into lightly, or simply to satisfy lust, but soberly and with understanding of the purposes of marriage: procreation and nurture of children, a remedy against sexual sin, and "the mutual society, help, and comfort that the one ought to have of the other, both in prosperity and adversity, into which holy state these two persons present, come now to be joined." The familiar biblical allusions from Genesis and Ephesians are joined with the less frequent (in the West) citation of John 2; also present are the traditional goods of marriage.[116]

The priest asks both the congregation and the couple whether there are any impediments to their marriage before asking for the consent of both man and woman. One recognizes echoes of the Sarum rite, now in the cadences of Cranmer's literary gift. The man promises to love, comfort, honor, and keep his wife; the woman promises to obey, serve, love, honor, and keep her husband, both of them forsaking all others as long as they both shall live. When each has answered in the affirmative, the priest asks, "Who giveth this woman to be married unto this man?" at which point her father or a friend presents her, and the two join right hands to pronounce their vows:

I, N., take thee, N.,
to be my wedded wife [husband],
to have and to hold from this day forward,
for better, for worse,
for richer, for poorer,
in sickness, and in health,
to love and to cherish, [the woman vows "to love, cherish,
    and to obey"]
till death us depart [1662: "till death us do part"];
according to God's holy ordinance,
and thereto I give thee my troth.

The man then gives the woman a ring. No longer, however, does he perform the traditional ritual of placing the ring on thumb, index finger, and middle finger while speaking a

Trinitarian formula; now, he places the ring on the woman's fourth finger and makes the following vow:

With this ring I thee wed:
with my body I thee worship:
and with all my worldly goods I thee endow.
In the name of the Father, and of the Son,
    and of the Holy Ghost.

The priest has not blessed the ring, as had been the custom, but instead he prays over the couple and speaks a version of Matthew 19:6: "Those whom God hath joined together, let no man put asunder." Afterward he pronounces them "man and wife together" and gives a final blessing. Then they proceed to the Lord's table, where more prayers are said before the reading of Scripture, the preaching of a sermon (which seems to be optional), and the celebration of Communion.[117]

Cranmer straddles the line between retaining Catholic forms (in which he relies heavily on Augustine with regard to sex) and Reformation influences. Marriage is "God's holy ordinance" but not a sacrament. Interestingly, Cranmer rephrases Matthew 19:5 so that it is directed at two particular people, rather than at the institution of marriage. In 1549, a couple are required to receive Communion on the day they married; in the 1662 revision, Communion is celebrated if it is "convenient."

By 1662 marriage becomes an "occasional office," rather than a rite that takes place in the midst of the community's worship. A wedding is to involve the couple, their family, their friends, and the priest. "In a sense," opines Gillian Varcoe, "this is what marriage has always been: the intervention of state and church in people's domestic arrangements is the anomaly."[118]

The dramatic events surrounding Henry VIII also led to a plethora of writings on marriage and its dissolution, both in England and on the Continent, including those of Thomas Becon (chaplain to Cranmer), Heinrich Bullinger, and Martin Bucer. All three affirmed the traditional goods of marriage while lifting up love and friendship as primary goals. Bucer went further in suggesting that divorce ought to be allowed simply on the basis of mutual consent of the couple, arguing that marriage is an earthly institution, and suggesting that the contracting and dissolving of marriages ought to be left to the state.[119]

The chief characteristics of the Anglican theology of marriage that took shape can be seen in the work of Becon, Bullinger, and Bucer. Each rejected the definition of marriage as a sacrament, the superiority of celibacy, and many canon laws regarding the forming and dissolving of marriages. Each emphasized mutual consent of the couple as well as consent of parents and community, as well as marriage in the church (for both clergy and laity), the ability to divorce under certain circumstances, and the understanding of marriage as a covenant between husband and wife and made before God.[120]

Anglican marriage rites continued in a cycle of reform. Queen Mary repealed much of the work just described, though Elizabeth restored nearly everything in 1559. During the seventeenth century, English theologians developed a new model of the household as a "little commonwealth" in which "marriage was at once a gracious symbol of the divine, a solemn covenant with one's spouse, and a social unit alongside church and state. . . . [that] served and symbolized the commonwealth— that is, the common good—of the couple, the children, the church, and the state."[121] Several shifts occurred: new ideas of equality upended traditional hierarchical views of family relationships; the "biblical duties" of spouses were reinterpreted as mutual "natural and contractual" responsibilities; marriages were to be voluntary contracts between free persons; and the commonwealth of the family could be dissolved if one spouse abused another.[122]

The Anglican commonwealth model of marriage turned out to be flexible enough—especially around questions of marriage—to make room for widely divergent views, and the

Book of Common Prayer has been the tie that links the world-wide Anglican communion. As time went on, the model grew increasingly liberal, and this is "the great irony of the Anglican contribution to the Western tradition of marriage." As Witte explains, "What began in the sixteenth century as the most conservative Christian tradition of marriage in all of Western Christendom ultimately gave birth to the most liberal Christian tradition of marriage three centuries later."[123]

The chief contribution of the commonwealth model was a radical democratization of husband and wife, parent and child, church and family—each relationship was defined with regard to the natural rights of each member of the household. Marriage laws gradually became more and more liberal—and laid the groundwork for the contractarian model of marriage that would emerge during the Enlightenment.

THE CATHOLIC RESPONSE

While various Protestant theologies and liturgies came into being, Catholic theologians continued to develop their own theological positions as well. With the Council of Trent came the definitive word: marriage was one of the seven sacraments, instituted by Jesus Christ and conferring grace. In so naming marriage as a sacrament, the council referred to Genesis 2:23–24, where Adam declares, "'This at last is bone of my bones and flesh of my flesh. . . .' Therefore a man leaves his father and mother and clings to his wife, and they become one flesh." When Christ refers to this text, the council reasoned, he considers it "words spoken by God," insisting therefore that "what God has joined together, let no man put asunder" (cf. Mark 10:9; Matt. 19:6). In doing so, the council declared, Christ "confirmed the stability of that same bond which had been declared by Adam so long before." As Christ instituted and perfected the sacraments, "he merited for us by his passion the grace that brings natural love to perfection, and strengthens the indissoluble unity, and sanctifies the spouses."[124] The grace given through the sacrament of marriage, then, is related to the union between Christ and the church that is expressed in Ephesians 5. That grace perfects the natural love that is between them and enables them to keep their marriage vows until death.[125]

With the Council of Trent also came the requirement that all couples marry in a Christian ceremony with a priest attending, using whatever liturgy was customary in that area.[126] Clandestine marriages were prohibited, since couples were required to be married in the presence of a priest and two witnesses.[127] By then marriage liturgies had developed in French-, Spanish-, and English-speaking countries, drawing from some of the same sources but also incorporating local customs. What became important in all liturgies, however, was the consent of both partners, spoken aloud in the vernacular and in the present tense (that is, not as a future promise); this became the most important element of the marriage liturgy.[128] The marriage vow, according to the Tridentine Catechism (1566), "is not a mere promise, but a transfer of right, by which the man actually yields the dominion of his body to the woman, the woman the dominion of her body to the man." Consummation, while expected to take place, was not required to validate the vows.[129]

Marriage was understood, then, as a contractual union as well as a natural union—that is, not a human invention, but one "instituted from the beginning to propagate the human race." At the same time, marriage was considered sacramental, an indissoluble union that is a symbol of Christ's everlasting union with the church, anticipated at creation and completed only with the return of Christ, and "a bond 'of the greatest affection and love.'"[130]

Finally, marriage became a public event. What had taken place primarily in the home now took place—at least for the upper classes—in the church. Banns were read several times, vows were made in public, and blessings once pronounced over the couple in the home were now spoken in the sanctuary. In spite of the church's insistence that couples marry in church, many people in the lower classes still got married without the involvement of clergy. While some marriages were blessed by the church, many people simply were married by virtue of the fact that they started living together. Nevertheless, as far as the theologians and canonists were concerned, the church became the place where marriages are made.[131] The Tridentine understanding of marriage endured until the late twentieth century, when the Second Vatican Council both confirmed and reconsidered its teaching.[132]

CONCLUSION

The traditions we have surveyed—the Catholic (sacramental), Lutheran, Calvinist, and Anglican—laid the foundation for future laws and liturgies of the church worldwide. This is a complicated story and fraught with the injustices of colonialism. The sacramental model of marriage thrived in Italy, France, Spain, and Portugal as well as their colonies, spreading to Latin America, the Caribbean islands, Louisiana, Quebec, and other settlements. Parts of Germany, Austria, Switzerland, and Scandinavia adopted the Lutheran social model, as did their colonies. The covenantal model that emerged from Calvinist Geneva was carried to Huguenot and Pietist communities in Western Europe as well as Puritan and Presbyterian groups in England and the American Colonies. The commonwealth model, of course, continued to dominate a good deal of Great Britain as well as its numerous colonies.[133]

With the eighteenth century and the rise of the Enlightenment, marriage came to be understood as a "voluntary bargain struck between two parties who wanted to come together into an intimate association." The people marrying determine the nature of their union—within the bounds of accepted laws and norms—but not the church, the government, family traditions, or community mores. As Witte puts it, "Couples should now be able to make their own marital beds and then to lie in them or leave them as they saw fit."[134] Eventually, social critics would call for the equality of men and women to hold property and to work, as well as reforms that would make annulment and divorce matters of the state rather than the church. By the twentieth century, a wave of legal changes in America and elsewhere allowed marriages to be formed and dissolved by civil, not ecclesial, government. Laws were passed regarding alimony, spousal and child abuse, and child custody, to name just a few. People began to consider issues regarding marriage and family as private matters; they may be governed by civil laws and informed by religious principles, but "neither the church nor the local community nor the paterfamilias could override the reasonable expressions of will of the marital parties themselves."[135]

Throughout the centuries, marriage has traveled from being a domestic contract to a churchly sacrament to a civil contract that may or may not have religious meaning. Within that overall pattern, however, is great complexity and variety. Churches worked out for themselves whether marriage is a heavenly estate or an earthly one, or a little bit of both. Theological debates were coupled with questions of jurisdiction—is the church responsible or the state? Or both? Sociological differences affect how the story is told as well. How the upper class made marriages did not necessarily reflect the practices of people in lower economic classes. While written liturgies give us a sense of the theology and practice of the churches, local pastors may or may not have known about them and surely improvised when circumstances required. Even when church authorities urged uniformity, local customs were often retained or they resurfaced. (Even today, for example, some brides want to be "given away," not because there is any transfer of property but because it is tradition.) In all of their complexity, all of the theological traditions we have discussed, and the liturgies they produced, have influenced, to some degree or another, how contemporary Christians think about marriage.

As we think about marriage in America in the twenty-first century and seek to define the church's role, we can pose the following observations:

- Marriage continues to involve both legal and ecclesial realms. Protestant churches are free to define for themselves whether and how they will participate in the legal matters pertaining to weddings. Clergy may sign marriage licenses as an expediency, or they may choose to confine their role to the spiritual and liturgical. Some couples—particularly same-gender couples who have only recently won the right to marry—prefer that their ministers sign marriage licenses as an affirmation of both their legal right and the recognition and blessing of the church.
- Households have taken different shapes throughout history and continue to do so. Rather than insist on a particular configuration of a family, the church does well to acknowledge the various ways people live together—cohabitation, remarriage after divorce, blended families, single-parent families, same-gender couples and their children, multigenerational families, and so forth. Acknowledging the various forms of contemporary families allows the church to speak meaningfully into the lives people are living, whether Christian or not, and affirm life-giving practices based on the gospel.
- Over the centuries, marriage-making moved from being a private and domestic affair to a public and, in some cases, ecclesial one. Here at the beginning of the twenty-first century, weddings are sometimes public,

sometimes private (consider the rise of small destination weddings, for example); sometimes in ballrooms, sometimes in churches; sometimes involving clergy, sometimes involving other sorts of presiders, including civil servants, friends ordained by an online entity for the occasion, and freelance celebrants. The church—and clergy—who stay in the marriage business must be clear on what it is they are offering. Is the church simply another wedding provider? Or does the church have something distinctive to give?

- The history of marriage tells a story of ever-increasing emphasis on mutuality and equality between spouses. Premarital counseling, wedding liturgies, and ongoing conversation regarding the practices of marriage must uphold those values, which are clearly based on the gospel.
- People have always experienced attraction, affection, and love—sometimes within marriage, sometimes not. Twenty-first-century Americans, while acknowledging that marrying affects one's economic status, expect a marriage to be based on love and to be a source of ongoing sexual and emotional satisfaction. More than at any other time in history, contemporary marriages offer the possibility for tremendous happiness. As a result, we are more likely than ever before to end a marriage that is not satisfying.

Americans have greater freedom regarding marriage than at any other time in history. We have also come to expect a great deal of marriage. But can marriage bear the weight of our expectations? Love, as Margaret Farley says, "is notoriously fickle, waxing and waning in ways we cannot always control." She continues:

All the laws proclaimed, even reinforced by sanctions, do not save us from our inabilities to live together in peace and in joy. Children do hold us to one another and to them, but we have massive evidence that they alone cannot save our marriages. . . . Sheer free choice—the "grit your teeth and do it" sort of choice—is so limited. We want to remain loving and faithful, peaceful and strong, utterly self-forgetful and devoted, in a relationship of marriage. This may be easily said, but not so easily done. If life with a particular other becomes intolerable—as it can become—it will not be made tolerable simply by choosing it so—not by controlling the other or even by controlling one's own self.[136]

In spite of her seeming pessimism, Farley is not ready to give up on marriage, however, and neither am I.

For all of the challenges facing married people, there is also the possibility for deep joy.

Being married has made me a better person. Being married has made me a better Christian. That said, being a Christian has made me a better marriage partner, and my husband and I have taught one another about grace along the way. Actually, Christ has taught us both more about grace and allowed us to catch a glimpse of Love (with a capital *L*)—the Love that will one day encompass us all.

For some people, including Christians, marriage loses any sense of covenant or joy. Sometimes marriage is not possible—perhaps there was never an opportunity, perhaps love was lost, or perhaps it is not legal to marry the person who is most loved. Life is messy, human beings are imperfect, and the church is not always the most helpful place to be when things start coming apart. Sometimes the body of Christ is just what it needs to be, but we have some work to do to make the church a place of hope, nurture, and redemption for those who would marry, those navigating the waters of marriage, as well as those for whom marriage has ended. It is to that task that we now turn.

Chapter 4

FEASTING AT THE TABLE OF LOVE

*Our bond is no little economy based on the exchange
of my love and work for yours, so much for so much
of an expendable fund. We don't know what its limits
are—that puts us in the dark. We are more together
than we know, how else could we keep on discovering
we are more together than we thought?*

—*Wendell Berry, "The Country of Marriage"*

ANYONE WHO HAS TRIED TO CHOOSE SCRIPTURE READINGS FOR A
wedding knows that the Bible does not say much about marriage—and that what it does say is not always helpful! Scripture
offers an array of models for marriage, including polygamy and
concubinage. Although God uses the marriage between Hosea
and Gomer to teach Israel about what a covenant looks like, no
one would consider their marriage one to emulate. Jesus, for
his part, says very little about marriage, although he apparently
did attend at least one wedding. Paul, as we have seen, would
prefer that people stay single if they can. While the household
code in Ephesians 5 may have hinted at a certain mutuality in
the marital relationship, many Christians cannot reconcile its
model for marriage with contemporary sensibilities. As Old
Testament scholar Ellen Davis said when quoting one of her
students, "The Bible doesn't always say what you thought it
did—or wish it did."[1] The truth is, no biblical writer could have
imagined marriage the way many American Christians understand it now—an egalitarian commitment between two people

who love each other and depend on one another for romance, sexual fulfillment, mutual support, and happiness.

At first glance, then, we might wonder whether Scripture has much to offer to contemporary Christians when it comes to understanding marriage. Yet we continue to affirm the authority of Scripture in our lives, even when it seems to run counter to what we know from our experience in the world. Even when we are offended by what we find in the Bible, we can remain open to it and allow ourselves to be changed by it. At the same time, however, we can disagree with what we find in the Bible, particularly since the biblical writers themselves disagree with one another. Yet disagreeing with a text is not based simply on our own opinions or predilections but is done in conversation with other Christians, in obedience to the overall witness of Scripture, and as part of the church's life of worship, study, and prayer.[2]

Since the time of Acts, Christians have sought to interpret Scripture for their own time. Indeed, the history of biblical interpretation shows that understandings of Scripture change because life changes. American Christians, for instance, no longer use the Bible to argue that slavery is God-ordained. In every age, people of faith trust the Holy Spirit to speak through the Bible—the living Word—into various circumstances. This means wrestling with Scripture's own historical contexts, acknowledging how the Word is spoken to people in different times and places in the biblical world while seeking wisdom for our own. Again, we must consider particular passages in light of the whole of Scripture.[3] When we use Scripture to interpret Scripture, we seek meaning in difficult passages by considering them in light of the gospel, including texts that might not seem to be specifically related to the text in question.[4] Such an approach helps ensure that we consider challenging texts as they relate to the whole biblical witness and opens us to the possibility that God will speak a new word for our lives.

In considering the church's role in weddings, it is important to look carefully at the passages of Scripture that consistently appear in treatises, sermons, and wedding services from the earliest Christian writings to contemporary liturgies. Six texts form what I call the "marriage canon"—those that have formed the way Christians have thought about marriage for the last two thousand years:

- Genesis 1:26–31 (male and female, made in God's image; "be fruitful and multiply")
- Genesis 2:18–24 (the two shall "become one flesh")
- 1 Corinthians 7:1–9 (it is better to marry than to burn)
- Ephesians 5:21–33 ("wives, be subject to your husbands"; "husbands, love your wives"; human marriage compared to the union of Christ and the church)
- Matthew 19:1–9 (Jesus' pronouncement against divorce; "what God has joined together, let no one separate")
- John 2:1–11 (Jesus turns water into wine at a wedding in Cana)

In this chapter I will note traditional understandings of these six passages and then explore how they speak into our own time. Second, I will enlarge the range of texts on which we depend to describe marriage between Christians and imagine what the church has to say to married people. Finally, I will consider how these texts lead us to understand marriage within the framework of eschatological hope, a framework that allows for both failure and forgiveness in light of Christ's all-encompassing grace.

MARRIAGE IN SCRIPTURE: HEARING CLASSIC TEXTS IN CONTEMPORARY TIMES

Genesis 1:26–31. In this first creation account, God creates humans in the image of God, blesses them, and commands them to "be fruitful and multiply," to fill the earth and to care for all of its creatures, and to feast upon its vegetation. At this point in the account, God's creation is "very good." There is much to say about this creation story and its implications for how we treat one another and the created order. For our purposes, however, we will focus on God's directions to the first humans. As noted in chapter 3, the command to "be fruitful and multiply" led early theologians to name the procreation and nurture of children as a primary purpose for—and benefit of—marriage. Contemporary Christians can certainly affirm that children represent one of God's greatest gifts. Yet many of those same Christians would be less likely to consider the making of children as the sole reason for marrying, or even the sole reason for sustaining a sexual relationship. As Roman Catholic ethicist Margaret Farley points out, being in relationship "does not end with the birth of children; it stretches to include the rearing of children, the initiation of new generations into a culture and civilization, and the ongoing building of the human community."[5] Furthermore, many couples cannot conceive children or choose not to do so. To consider procreation a chief purpose of marriage is to negate the validity and value of families without children. Couples who bear children through donor insemination or surrogacy, or those who adopt, certainly provide nurture for children without the act of procreation. Those concerned with the sustainability of planet Earth caution against unbridled population growth. How then can we understand the command to "be fruitful and multiply"? Finally, to consider procreation as a chief end of marriage is to deny the possibility of marriage to older couples as well as same-gender couples.

Some twenty-first-century theologians argue that "fruitfulness" can be understood in a variety of ways; bearing and raising children is but one way that a couple might be fruitful. A marriage that is not fruitful, in fact, turns in on itself. As Farley puts it:

The new life within the relationship of those who share it may move beyond itself in countless ways: nourishing other relationships; providing goods, services, and beauty for others; informing the fruitful work lives of the partners in relation; helping to raise other people's children; and on and on. All of these ways and more may constitute the fruit of a love for which persons in relation are responsible. . . . Interpersonal love, then, and perhaps in a special way, sexual love insofar as it is just, must be fruitful.[6]

Ghanaian theologian Mercy Amba Oduyoye—who has no biological children and for years struggled to come to terms with the expectations of her family and the wider culture in which she lived—describes her vision of fruitfulness this way:

Increase in humanity.
Multiply the likeness to God for which you have the potential.
Multiply the fullness of humanity that is found in Christ.
Fill the earth with the glory of God.
Increase in creativity.
Bring into being that which God can look upon and pronounce "good," even "very good."[7]

Every marriage, then, regardless of whether or not biological children are produced, has the potential to be eminently fruitful. The divine command invites us into God's work of creating—by birthing and nurturing children, yes, but also through all sorts of life-giving, life-sustaining acts.

This view is reflected in contemporary marriage liturgies, which are more circumspect when it comes to mentioning children and their importance to marriage. The 1979 *Book of Common Prayer* of the Episcopal Church, for example, eliminated the assertion that procreation is the primary purpose of marriage, focusing instead on the "mutual joy" of the partners and the "help and comfort" they give to one another. A marriage service from the United Church of Canada states that marriage "enables two people to share their desires, longings, dreams, and memories, and to help each other through their uncertainties."

An optional sentence mentions children but does not assume that those children are biologically related to the marrying couple: "United as one, the two may provide the love and support in which children grow and flourish."[8]

Genesis 2:18–24. In this second creation story, God declares that it is not good for the human to be alone. Already companionship is built into the fabric of life; to be human is to be in community. The word "marriage" is never used here, but some sort of kinship is understood. "Together, they form a community of correspondence," says William Brown, "enjoying mutual companionship and help."[9] What was "not good" is now "good"—humans were created to live in relationship with one another. This new creature, woman, is created as a "suitable helper" for the man; the Hebrew phrase does not imply a subordinate but a companion who provides mutual support.[10]

When the man sees his new companion for the first time, he recognizes another being who is made of the same stuff and erupts in poetic speech:

> This at last is bone of my bones
> and flesh of my flesh;
> this one shall be called Woman,
> for out of Man this one was taken.
> (Gen. 2:23)

Some of the early marriage liturgies considered in chapter 3 reflected the notion that woman, having been fashioned from the rib of man, is therefore derivative, or weaker. Yet as Walter Brueggemann has argued, the implications of the Hebrew text suggest otherwise. The noun *bsr* means "flesh," both in the sense of meat (that is, physicality) and in the sense of frailty. The closest English translation is "flesh-weakness." Similarly, the word translated as "bone" is related to might; it is best rendered as "bone-power." Taken together, "flesh-weakness" and "bone-power" voice a whole range of conditions from strength to weakness. The relationship between the first two humans "is one which is affirmed for every possible contingency in the relationship, as we affirm in the marriage formula, 'in sickness and in health, in plenty and in want,'" explains Brueggemann. "It is a formula of constancy, of abiding loyalty which in the first place has nothing to do with biological derivation, as it is often interpreted."[11] In other words, this is covenant language, an expression of "profound loyalty and solidarity of purpose." It is, in essence, an oath to share together in the purpose God gives to humans, caring for the earth.[12]

To speak of marriage in terms of a covenant is to speak of living in a committed relationship marked by *hesed*, or steadfast love. When people live in covenant with one another, they imitate God's own faithfulness and steadfast love toward God's people.[13] Although Scripture describes a variety of forms of covenant, in applying the term to marriage it is assumed that this covenant is mutual and egalitarian.

The author of Genesis goes on to say, "Therefore a man leaves his father and his mother and clings to his wife, and they become one flesh" (v. 24). This verse refers to a pattern of human life involving fathers, mothers, and children that will eventually take shape. It serves, therefore, as an etiology of marriage—that is, an explanation regarding the origins of marriage—that connects "God's original intention for creation and later practice."[14] Two people leave their families to form another, forging a bond of fidelity and mutual support. For the author of Genesis, leaving one's parents usually means marriage, and marriage includes physical intimacy, but "one flesh," Brueggemann argues, refers primarily to kinship rather than "biological derivation or sexual intercourse."[15] The focus is on solidarity and fidelity; the oaths humans make are set against the backdrop of God's covenant with God's people. From the beginning, Israel "knew she lived in a world where solidarity, fidelity, and responsibility are the essentials of *shalom*."[16]

A further implication of Genesis 2:18–24 is that such a bond of fidelity can be made between any two people. Certainly the male-female relationship is presented here as foundational, but there is nothing that precludes persons of the same gender taking oaths of mutual support and loyalty. As Patrick Miller explains, no line is drawn that excludes relationships other than male-female; in fact, the creation story "stresses plurality, fullness, and the rich variety of God's creative power."[17]

It should be noted that talk of marriage as reflecting the divine-human covenant must challenge any sense that one marriage partner is superior and the other subordinate. As Margaret Farley points out, a marriage ethic rooted in justice is attentive to the problems of domestic violence and other forms of physical or emotional abuse. "Everyone can see the problem with harming one another, especially in the close situations of family relationships," she says. "But not everyone sees the relevance of power differentials in families, or how violence can rise from a sense of powerlessness effected by religiously inspired but unrealistic expectations placed on persons in family roles."[18] With this caution in mind, we can draw on covenantal language to inform a theologically sound understanding of marriage for our time.

"Covenant" suggests a deep and mutual agreement, a commitment to persevere grounded in divine wisdom and power and not only in the civil order. Covenant also implies the promise of both human and divine faithfulness devoted to the upholding and strengthening of the relationship. Those who enter a contract make an agreement that is upheld by the civil authorities (represented in the United States by a marriage license). Those who form a covenant, however, do more than transact a legal agreement. They form a bond, a commitment that implies emotional and even spiritual fidelity and dedication, one that is witnessed and upheld by God. The contractual model emphasizes self-interest and risk avoidance and stipulates a time frame. In contrast, the covenantal model involves commitment to the other, acknowledges risk, and assumes an ongoing relationship. Furthermore, "the covenant mentality replenishes romantic love with unconditional love . . . [where] each resolves before God to cherish the other in mutual self-affirmation and giving."[19] When covenantal language is described in this way—without the references to divine-human covenants and their power differentials—then the Christian understanding of marriage is rooted in the mutuality that is implied in the Genesis text.

1 Corinthians 7:1–9. "Paul, Paul, Paul, Paul . . . You hopeless romantic." So begins a sermon by Presbyterian minister Brian Ellison, who goes on to suggest slogans that could be adopted after reading this passage:

> "Marriage—Better Than Being On Fire"
> "Marriage—Not So Bad (Since the World Will End Soon)"
> "Marriage—Like a Course of Antibiotics, You Should Finish
>   If You've Already Started"[20]

It is hard to imagine that this section of Paul's letter has much to say to contemporary Christians. Yet Ellison points out that "the faith community of Corinth . . . was one where sexual ethics and family arrangements were but one battleground in a rapidly evolving new world, where the church had no choice but to make up its answers on the fly because the questions were changing so fast." Looking at his hearers, Ellison asks, "Sound familiar?"[21]

As discussed in chapter 3, Paul responds to the Corinthians' questions about sex and marriage in light of his conviction that Christ would soon return. "It is well for a man not to touch a woman," they wrote to him, questioning whether they should be marrying at all. He responds by telling them not to disrupt their lives—the married folks should stay married and keep having sex so that no one is tempted to seek intercourse with someone outside the marriage. Widows and widowers should remain unmarried, and the unmarried should stay that way, in light of Christ's imminent arrival, unless not being married leads them to sexual sin. Paul's response reflects an ethic of mutuality: wives and husbands are both instructed to make their bodies available to their mates. Furthermore, each has authority over the other's body. Marriage is good, and sexual relations between married people are good. Paul gives his best advice, trusting that whatever decisions people make for themselves, they will be ready for Christ when he comes.

As we have seen, this passage has been used to assert that celibacy is a superior way of life—an assertion rejected by the Protestant Reformers and, more recently, by some Roman Catholic theologians as well. Indeed, some Protestant and Catholic thinkers are considering how celibacy might inform marriage. Kathleen Norris, a Presbyterian author who has sojourned frequently with the Benedictines, compares living as a celibate to living in monogamy. "What distinguished all the Benedictine women that I spoke with from most of the married people I know is how consistently they spoke of celibacy as being rooted in the religious, as 'having gospel value,' or of 'being a sign of the kingdom.'" Perhaps churches fail to emphasize the "sacredness of a lifelong commitment," she suggests, "whereas for sisters the religious nature of their vows is an everyday reality."[22] One sister told Norris, "One needs a deep prayer life to maintain a celibate life. It is only through prayer that the hard choices get made, over time, only prayer that can give me the self-transcendence that celibacy requires." What difference would it make for married people to keep their vows with such intentionality each day? It would, indeed, be a matter of prayer. As Norris points out, self-transcendence is necessary in marriage, too. Yet the culture in which we live perpetuates the idea that love is about possession of another. Celibacy, on the other hand, "seeks to love non-exclusively, non-possessively."[23]

Anglican theologian Sarah Coakley points out that long, faithful marriages actually require couples to be celibate from time to time—during a difficult pregnancy, for instance, or around the time of childbirth, when a partner falls ill or becomes impotent, or during periods of physical separation. "The reflective, faithful celibate and the reflective, faithful married person may have more in common—by way of prayerful surrendering of inevitably thwarted desire to God—than the unreflective or faithless celibate, or the carelessly happy, or indeed unhappily careless, married person."[24] Celibacy, in whatever circumstance, requires setting aside self-interest and focusing on giving of one's self to another.

All of life, then—including our most intimate relationships—is caught up in our devotion to Jesus Christ. Some of us live out our Christian vocation through a celibate life; some of us do so, at least in part, through a married life. Physical desire is not problematic in and of itself; many theologians see it as a symptom of our desire for union with God. Yet it is bridled by an ethic of mutual care and respect and channeled through relationships of love, sexual or otherwise.

Brian Ellison's sermon ends this way:

> The reason we, in our faith and practice of marriage, embody abundance and not asceticism, faithful embrace and not fearful resistance, is that in this "earthly ordinance" and in every other whether we are married or not, we all fulfill our vocation, and so live into the life that is ours in Jesus Christ. So let us tear off the bumper stickers and strip away the restrictions that diminish or demean God's calling to all. And let us in humility pray that all our living as individuals and as the church would glorify God.[25]

Ephesians 5:21–33. It is tempting to dismiss this passage of Scripture as hopelessly anachronistic and of no value to contemporary couples. Wives are exhorted to be subject to their husbands, whatever the circumstance, and husbands, while instructed to love their wives in Christ-like fashion, are still in charge! Furthermore, the advice given to spouses is part of a larger household code in which masters and slaves are also addressed, causing some twenty-first-century Christians to question the value of the entire passage. Yet in spite of language that sounds oppressive to many contemporary hearers, we seek to hear the text with charity and discern a gospel word.

Although the author of Ephesians instructs his hearers to renounce pagan ways in the first twenty verses of chapter 5, in this passage he advises them how to best live within the conventional household arrangements of the time. In one sense, he takes a conservative stance: live within the hierarchical structures that you know. In another sense, however, the Christians at Ephesus heard a surprising word as well: all members of the household—regardless of gender, age, or status—are to "be subject to one another out of reverence for Christ" (Eph. 5:21). So, then, it may not be surprising to hear wives (or children or slaves) exhorted to serve or submit, but it is unusual to hear the same injunction directed at husbands.[26]

Nevertheless, one would not call this text liberative. Even if it did hold some sense of mutuality for first-century couples, the emphasis is still on woman's submission and man's lordship. For some women, this text squelches any sense of equality in a marriage; for some men, this text justifies controlling—and even abusive—behavior. This text also encourages some women to stay in marriages that are damaging and even dangerous. Even a troublesome text, however, can impart good news. As Frances Taylor Gench points out, the author of Ephesians seeks to show how the faith helps Christians know how to treat one another—something contemporary Christians also seek to do. She notes, too, that husbands are instructed not once, but three times (vv. 25, 28, 33), to love their wives rather than dominate them. "Love is more than that emotion extolled in Hallmark-speak as 'the feeling you feel when you feel you're going to feel a feeling you've never felt before,'" she says. "Love, for the author of Ephesians, is defined by Jesus Christ and through the lens of the cross."[27] This text speaks into a social context—and a household structure—that is far different from our own, reminding us that in every century Christians have sought to understand how the gospel informs, even shapes, our life together.

New Testament scholar E. Elizabeth Johnson argues that the author of Ephesians backs away from the more radical egalitarianism of Paul and adheres more closely to the model of a patriarchal household common in his time. As a result, women do not hear of the equality that comes with the new creation that they heard in the preaching of Paul (cf. Gal. 3:28; 2 Cor. 5:17, Gal. 6:15).[28] For this reason, then, we must consider Ephesians 5:21–33 in light of those texts that proclaim that all who are baptized are one in Jesus Christ. Paul's insistence that there is no more male and female (hearkening back to the description in Gen. 1:27 that man and woman were made in God's image) provides an important counterbalance to the hierarchy implied in the Ephesians text. By putting these two texts in conversation with one another, we avoid seeing the Bible as an array of independent texts that offer up "discrete bits of theological truth. . . . The Bible's witness is cumulative, with the authority of any one part also determined by its relation to the whole."[29] The church trusts Scripture to speak into its lived experience through the power of the Holy Spirit, who enables the good news of Jesus Christ to be proclaimed in every time and place.

Toward the end of the passage, the author of Ephesians asserts that a husband is to love his wife as he does his own body—and as Christ loves the church. Quoting Genesis 2:24, he draws on the metaphor of "one flesh," therefore linking the bond between Christ and the church with God's covenant of loyalty with Israel.[30] Once again, caution is required. To compare human marriage to Christ's bond to the church is to hold up a standard that human beings can never achieve.[31] As we shall soon see, this will have implications for an eschatological understanding of marriage.

Matthew 19:1–9. "What God has joined together, let no one separate." These words, recorded in the Gospels of Mark and Matthew, have long appeared (in one form or another) in wedding liturgies. They affirm the confidence that God is involved in the joining of two people in marriage and serve as a reminder that no one should interfere in that divine work. But do those words belong in a marriage rite? Certainly, most people who make vows to live in marriage "till death do us part" intend to honor those vows. But, as we have seen, roughly half of all people who say those words break the promises they make. Not all marriages are full of blessing; some are dishonored by physical or emotional abuse, others are marred by a failure to live up to vows of fidelity. Christian people enter marriage under all sorts of circumstances, and one must ask whether we can assume that God has "joined together" all of these unions. Furthermore, there are times when one must consider it possible that *God* is the one who separates couples who have been married.[32] So what do we do with this saying?

It is helpful to consider the context in which Jesus speaks these words. He is responding to a question from some Pharisees who want to know whether a man can divorce his wife for any reason. They hope he will weigh in on a rabbinical debate regarding Deuteronomy 24:1 ("Suppose a man enters into marriage with a woman, but she does not please him because he finds something objectionable about her, and so he writes her a certificate of divorce, puts it in her hand, and sends her out of his house . . ."). One school argues that the "something objectionable" is infidelity, while another school argues that a man can divorce his wife for any cause. Rather than settle their dispute, however, Jesus changes the question. He quotes Genesis 1:27 and 2:24, reminding them that God "made them male and female" and that "'for this reason a man shall leave his father and mother and be joined to his wife, and the two shall become one flesh.' . . . Therefore what God has joined together, let no one separate" (Matt. 19:4–6; cf. Mark 10:6–9). Jesus is not defining the circumstances in which divorce is legal, but rather affirming God's intention that people live in companionship with one another.[33]

The Pharisees' question—while not identical to our own questions about divorce—enables us to hear from Jesus wisdom regarding God's intentions for humankind. The answer is not to define whether Christians should be allowed to divorce; it is, instead, to affirm the divine provision for humans to live in intimate companionship with one another. So if "let no one put asunder" is said at weddings, it must somehow be expressed as an affirmation that God desires mutually loving relationships for us and not as a moralistic pronouncement. We can say, with the author of Hebrews, "Let marriage be held in honor by all" (Heb. 13:4) while allowing that marriages do sometimes end and that the human capacity for love falls short of the divine capacity.

John 2:1–11. Contemporary Christians can take delight in the fact that Jesus was a guest at a wedding one day in the Galilean town of Cana. It may seem curmudgeonly to insist that just because Jesus once attended a wedding does not mean that he blessed the institution of marriage, as is sometimes claimed in marriage liturgies. Nowhere does Jesus discuss the wedding at hand or offer thoughts on marriage. Jesus' miracle of turning water into wine—exceptional wine at that!—offers no commentary on marriage but rather is the first "sign" (*semeion*) that points to his divine identity. We can, however, affirm that Christ's presence was a blessing to that particular wedding—and that we trust him to be present at our own weddings, too, as expressed in the following prayer from *Evangelical Lutheran Worship*:

Eternal God,
our creator and redeemer,
as you gladdened the wedding
at Cana in Galilee
by the presence of your Son,
so bring your joy to this wedding by his presence now.
Look in favor upon *name* and *name* and grant that they,
rejoicing in all your gifts,
may at length celebrate
the unending marriage feast
with Christ our Lord,
who lives and reigns with you
and the Holy Spirit, one God,
now and forever.[34]

To pray for the gladdening presence of Christ is to acknowledge the sacramental nature of marriage. Even those who do not consider it a dominical sacrament—that is, one commanded by Christ—can view marriage in general, and weddings in particular, as places where Christ is made known to us.

When Jesus turns water into wine, he gives the wedding guests a taste of the glory to come. This wine is exquisite, to be sure, but it is nothing in comparison to the wine to be served at the marriage supper of the Lamb (Rev. 19:6–9a). A wedding also points to the joy that is promised to us all when Christ comes again. As Presbyterian minister Kim Clayton once put it, "From the start of John's gospel we learn that with Jesus, there is always *more* and *better* still to come. Isn't this the message, the hope of every wedding? That the exquisite beauty and overflowing love of the wedding day is only the beginning of more and better still to come."[35]

At its best, a marriage can do the same; a moment of deep joy or an experience of grace can give us a glimpse of complete union and overwhelming love.

MARRIAGE IN SCRIPTURE: EXPANDING THE RANGE OF TEXTS

Having considered the six foundational texts of the marriage canon, we now turn to other biblical passages that might inform twenty-first-century Christians. At the heart of it, marriage is a kind of human relationship. Although we have seen that the Bible says very little about marriage as we know it, Scripture does say a great deal about how to live in right relationship with God and one another. For Christians, marriage is a sphere (though not the only sphere) where two people work out their salvation together, struggling to grow more and more in the likeness of Christ while trying not to burn dinner and learning how to fight fairly.

Not surprisingly, the epistles give us texts that help us understand how to best do that. Paul's Letter to the Romans includes an exhortation to live as a Christian that is, perhaps, the best instruction for marriage in all of Scripture:

> Let love be genuine; hate what is evil, hold fast to what is good;
> love one another with mutual affection; outdo one another in
>   showing honor.
> Do not lag in zeal, be ardent in spirit, serve the Lord.
> Rejoice in hope, be patient in suffering, persevere in prayer.
> Contribute to the needs of the saints; extend hospitality to
>   strangers.
>
> Bless those who persecute you; bless and do not curse them.
> Rejoice with those who rejoice, weep with those who weep.
> Live in harmony with one another; do not be haughty,
> but associate with the lowly;
> do not claim to be wiser than you are.
> Do not repay anyone evil for evil,
> but take thought for what is noble in the sight of all.
> If it is possible, so far as it depends on you,
> live peaceably with all.
>
> (Rom. 12:9–18)

The first part of this passage describes mutual self-giving while hinting at the sort of joy that might come from "outdoing" one another in honoring, loving, delighting. The text includes other advice for living together as well; "live in harmony" and "do not claim to be wiser than you are" are useful instructions for any human relationship, and especially for marriage.

The text also takes an outward turn; those who are married are encouraged to treat *all* people this way. The couple who are married decide together to look out for the needs of others and to show hospitality, to share in the joys and sorrows of others, and to seek peace—in short, to live out their baptismal vocations.

From the beginning, marriage was considered Christian because it was the joining of two baptized believers in Jesus Christ. It wasn't the wedding that made the marriage Christian, it was their baptisms.[36] When Christians marry, they decide to go on a pilgrimage of sorts, to live out their baptismal vocation together. When the Episcopal Church set out to study marriage and develop a resource for blessing same-sex marriages, it began with the church's focus on mission, rooted in baptism, "which incorporates us into the Body of Christ and commissions us to participate in God's mission of reconciliation in the world (2 Cor. 5:17–19)."[37] This mission seeks to restore all people to "unity with God and with each other in Christ."[38] When Christians marry, they take part in this mission by living as disciples and "witnessing to Christ in how we live in our closest relationships."[39]

Biblical texts that speak to our baptismal identity can also help us to see how Christians might live out their vocation in and through marriage. The Letter to the Colossians, for example, includes a lyrical passage that all Christians—and indeed, all married couples—should commit to memory:

As God's chosen ones, holy and beloved, clothe yourselves
    with compassion,
kindness, humility, meekness, and patience.
Bear with one another and, if anyone has a complaint against
    another,
forgive each other;
just as the Lord has forgiven you, so you also must forgive.
Above all, clothe yourselves with love,
which binds everything together in perfect harmony.

(Col. 3:12–14)

This text, which is sometimes spoken as a charge at the end
of a wedding service, imparts great wisdom to those who would
stay married. Certainly compassion, kindness, humility, meekness, and patience are all components of a loving relationship.
Even more, perhaps, is the baptismal language that the author
subtly employs. Many early Christians were baptized naked;
they turned their backs to the west, descended into the water,
and came up facing the east, new creations who were then
clothed in garments from Christ's own closet. In baptism we
are made holy because Christ himself is holy. We are clothed
in his righteousness, and only because we put on Christ can we
begin to imitate him in our own lives—and in our marriages.
One might say that this text points us to some important practices for marriage: compassion, kindness, humility, meekness,
patience, and, especially, forgiveness.

Cultivating forgiveness as a daily habit may be the single
most important thing married people can do. When we forgive one another on a daily basis—for leaving wet footprints
on the bathroom floor or forgetting to pay a bill on time—we
are better equipped to forgive one another for more serious
infractions and more readily able to heal the wounds that partners invariably inflict upon one another. Jean Vanier, founder
of L'Arche Community, insists that forgiveness is more than
simply saying "I forgive you." It involves seeking to understand
what lies behind hurtful words or destructive behavior. "To

forgive is to recognize once again—after separation—the covenant which binds us together," he says; it is to open oneself to the other once again. "It is to give them space in our hearts. That is why it is never easy to forgive. We too must change. We must learn to forgive and forgive and forgive every day, day after day. We need the power of the Holy Spirit in order to open up like that."[40]

A story I heard so many years ago is still emblazoned on my memory. Corrie ten Boom tells of coming face to face, many years later, with one of her jailers from the concentration camp at Ravensbruck. He was one of the soldiers who stood guard in the shower room, witness to the female prisoners' humiliation. Sometime after the war, she spoke at a church service about her experiences and preached about the overwhelming grace of God. Following the service, the former guard approached her, smiling, to thank her for her sermon. "How grateful I am for your message, *Fraulein,*" he said. "To think that, as you say, he has washed my sins away!" He put his hand forward to shake hers, but she could not return the gesture. Rage tore through her and she could only pray for help: "Jesus, I cannot forgive him. Give me your forgiveness." Somehow, through a power not her own, she raised her hand to shake that of the former soldier, and a remarkable thing happened:

> From my shoulder along my arm and through my hand a current seemed to pass from me to him, while into my heart sprang a love for this stranger that almost overwhelmed me. And so I discovered that it is not on our forgiveness any more than on our goodness that the world's healing hinges, but on His. When he tells us to love our enemies, He gives, along with the command, the love itself.[41]

This sort of forgiveness is not of the everyday variety, but it does point to the source of our ability to forgive, Jesus Christ. The love of God, from which nothing can separate us, is the spring from which our own forgiveness wells up. It does not overlook wrongdoing, but it chooses reconciliation over brokenness. Martin Luther King Jr. put it this way: "Forgiveness does not mean ignoring what has been done or putting a false label on an evil act. It means, rather, that the evil act no longer remains as a barrier to the relationship. Forgiveness is a catalyst creating the atmosphere necessary for a fresh start and a new beginning. It is the lifting of a burden or the canceling of a debt." So then, forgiveness does not mean that one holds on to the memory of the wrongdoing, nursing the hurt or stockpiling ammunition for some future disagreement. Nor does it mean that we forget all about it as though it did not matter; forgetting is not always possible. Rather, as King says, "we forget in the sense that the evil deed is no longer a mental block impeding a relationship."[42] And so contemporary marriage liturgies often include a prayer such as this from the *Book of Common Prayer*: "Give them grace, when they hurt each other, to recognize and acknowledge their fault, and to seek each other's forgiveness and yours."[43]

We may count Paul's instruction to the Galatians as part of the foundation for understanding marriage between Christians as well. To the baptized he writes, "There is no longer Jew or Greek, there is no longer slave or free, there is no longer male and female; for all of you are one in Christ Jesus" (Gal. 3:27–28). Reflected in his words is the unity between people regardless of sex, background, or class and, by implication, the sense of equality with which Christians ought to regard each other and, indeed, all people they meet. Furthermore, since unity is inextricable from the need to work for justice, Christians live out their call together. This is why, for instance, the Byzantine marriage liturgy includes a prayer for blessings on the couple that are "poured out, pressed down and running over," not only for the benefit of the couple, but for that of others, too: "Fill their houses with wheat grain and oil and with every good thing, so that they may give in turn to those in need."[44] One might say that for Christians who marry, there is no divide between the secular and the sacred—that is, between their lives lived together as married people and their lives lived together as disciples of Christ. "The renewal of Christian marriage," insist two prominent scholars of the history and theology of marriage, "would seem to be inseparable, finally, from the renewal of baptismal consciousness and from the profound consequences that will flow therefrom."[45]

When my family moved to Atlanta and visited for the first time the church we would eventually join, we were greeted by Margaret and Howard Montgomery. Their warmth was genuine; they made us feel as though our showing up that day was a source of delight and made us feel at home immediately. In the years that followed, I watched them do the same for countless other people and, indeed, saw them live out their witness to Jesus Christ in many other ways. It would be impossible to tell where their Christian vocation left off and their marriage began. Who is to say where the line would be drawn between how their marriage was a blessing to them and how it was the same to others? Who could say how their faith grew their marriage as well as their life in the world, or how their shared discipleship enriched their marriage? Their bond not only brought the two of them great happiness; it also was generative and gave witness to the love of God in Christ that seeks peace and justice for all. It is this sort of marriage that comes to mind when one hears this prayer spoken at a wedding:

> Make their life together a sign of Christ's love
> to this sinful and broken world,
> that unity may overcome estrangement,
> forgiveness heal guilt,
> and joy conquer despair.[46]

So faith shapes the contours of a marriage, and marriage, in turn, can grow faith, as a couple turns inward, and outward, in a dance of grace.

There is a sense in which marriage is the place where our baptism is lived out most intentionally and intimately and, perhaps, intensely. There was a time in my life when I thought being married meant you could save all your worst stuff for your spouse. Although I never quite subscribed to the famous line from the 1970s movie *Love Story*—"Love means never having to say you're sorry"—I did at some unconscious level think that you did not have to be careful with your words or actions with a partner, because that person would understand all of your weaknesses. Of course I had it all wrong. It is within our closest relationships, especially marriage, that we are called to bring our best, to live out the gospel as deeply, freely, and lovingly as we know how. Even more, we are called to rely on the power of the Holy Spirit to sanctify our marriages—that is, to lead us into ever-deepening ways of love.

Christian faith, then, informs marriage by teaching us to love and calling us to live out our baptismal vocations.

Scripture also invites us into joy. From the rhapsodic language extolling the beauty of each partner to the expressions of longing and expectation, the Song of Songs expresses the bodily delights of the lovers. Says one lover to another:

> How fair and pleasant you are,
>   O loved one, delectable maiden!
> You are stately as a palm tree,
>   and your breasts are like its clusters.
> I say I will climb the palm tree
>   and lay hold of its branches.
> O may your breasts be like clusters of the vine,
>   and the scent of your breath like apples,
> and your kisses like the best wine
>   that goes down smoothly,
>   gliding over lips and teeth.

The response comes:

I am my beloved's,
    and his desire is for me.
Come, my beloved,
    let us go forth into the fields
    and lodge in the villages;
let us go out early to the vineyards,
    and see whether the vines have budded,
whether the grape blossoms have opened
    and the pomegranates are in bloom.
There I will give you my love.
The mandrakes give forth fragrance,
    and over our doors are all choice fruits,
new as well as old,
    which I have laid up for you, O my beloved.
                                    (Song 7:6–13)

Both partners share in praising the charms of the other, both express desire for the other; neither seems to take a dominant role. After centuries of allegorical interpretation, many contemporary scholars agree that the Song of Songs is, at least in part, a poem spoken between two lovers who revel in their sexual relationship.[47] In contrast to some of the early Christian writings we have seen, where sex is treated with a certain amount of suspicion and celibacy is considered preferable to marriage, here we see physical intimacy as a gift that two people share, a gift characterized by mutual adoration and self-giving.

The *mutuality* of this self-giving cannot be overly stressed. We are not talking about the sort of mutuality that Jerry Maguire (played by Tom Cruise) described to his wife (Renée Zellweger) when he murmured, "You complete me."[48] This is not about needing your other half so you can be a whole person, or the kind of self-sacrifice that has, historically, been expected of women, the kind that leads to a devaluing of one person for the sake of another. Here is a picture of lovers freely giving themselves to one another.

The love poetry of the Song of Songs is as impassioned as

any—even erotic at times—but this is no top-40 love song or a lighthearted fling. The intensity of the love and commitment between the lovers is expressed with power and eloquence:

> Set me as a seal upon your heart,
>   as a seal upon your arm;
> for love is strong as death,
>   passion fierce as the grave.
> Its flashes are flashes of fire,
>   a raging flame.
> Many waters cannot quench love,
>   neither can floods drown it.
> If one offered for love
>   all the wealth of one's house,
>   it would be utterly scorned.
>   (8:6–7)

These words echo the covenant bond established in Genesis and foreshadow the eternal passion into which we are all called, allowing lovers here and now a taste of the love that one day will overwhelm us all.

We could consider still other texts that might inform our understandings of marriage. There is the story of the extraordinary fidelity between Ruth and Naomi, who redefine the meaning of family and display uncommon loyalty. We might draw on John's Gospel, where Jesus proclaims, "I am the vine, you are the branches. Those who abide in me and I in them bear much fruit" (15:5), to deepen our understanding of how a loving marriage is enabled by Christ. And although it is well established that 1 Corinthians 13 has nothing directly to do with marriage, it still speaks to the minds and hearts of those who marry.

Perhaps most significant, however, is a common thread that is glimpsed throughout the passages we have considered so far—the eschatological hope upon which marriage is based—and the practices that enable us to live into that hope. It is to this theme that we now turn.

MARRIAGE AND ESCHATOLOGICAL HOPE

In one way or another, each of the passages we have considered points us toward acknowledging two things: our inability to live up to God's good intentions for us and the hope we have in Jesus Christ, who even now redeems us and tethers us to the promise of the new creation. In Genesis 1, humans are made in the image of God, commanded to be fruitful, and entrusted with the care of creation. Yet we have failed to honor the image of God in ourselves and in others; we have filled the planet in such a way that there is great poverty, injustice, and oppression; we have defiled the earth, its skies, and its seas. We are a people in need of redemption.

In the second creation account, when God discovers that it is not good for the human being to be alone, a companion is created. People were meant to live in community with one another. We were made for companionship, and this first human relationship was designed with mutual support in mind as the two worked together to care for the created world. It did not take long for things to go wrong. Yet in the first human relationship is reflected the covenant that God intends with God's people—one of fidelity. We may not be able to keep covenant with one another, but God keeps covenant with us. God's fidelity assures us of grace when we fail to live up to God's intentions in our own relationships. God's faithfulness gives us hope that we might continually aspire to live more faithfully.

At first glance, Paul's First Letter to the Corinthians seems to be about earthly problems—to marry or not to marry, to engage in sexual relations or not—but at the heart of it all is Paul's concern that Christ's followers, whatever their marital state, be ready for his return. Christ is coming again, and Christians are called to live expectantly.

The Letter to the Ephesians points out that even in our time, we do not treat one another with mutual self-giving; we cannot come close to loving one another the way Christ loves the church.[49] And yet there is hope; our marriages may not fully reflect the sort of union that exists (and will come to completion) between Christ and the church, but even now we live into that promise that we will indeed be one with him. Even now our assumptions about who wields power and who serves are constantly challenged by a footwashing Lord,[50] one who has invited us into his own mystery.

Jesus speaks clearly against divorce. But it happens—sometimes unjustly, sometimes for good reasons, almost always painfully. Divorce is a result of our human condition; we are incapable of ever fully keeping covenant. Yet in his teaching regarding divorce, Jesus is most concerned with justice, not establishing unbreakable rules. He has a way of pointing to those things we cannot do: "it is easier for a camel to go through the eye of a needle than for someone who is rich to enter the kingdom of God" (Matt. 19:24). It may be easier for a camel to go through the eye of a needle than for a divorced person to enter the kingdom of God, too, but with God, Jesus reminds us, all things are possible.

Finally, at the wedding at Cana Jesus embodies the "more" and "better" that awaits us. Even the most joyful occasions—like weddings—show the cracks and fissures in human relationships. Nerves are frayed. Personalities are problematic. The wine runs out. Yet Jesus takes the ordinary stuff of our messy lives and transforms it into something better. Something more. Something that gives us a taste of what is yet to come.

Perhaps, then, one of the most important passages of Scripture to inform our understanding of marriage is from the book of Revelation, where John of Patmos describes hearing "the voice of a great multitude, like the sound of many waters and like the sound of mighty thunderpeals, crying out,

"Hallelujah!
For the Lord our God the Almighty reigns.

Let us rejoice and exult and give him the glory,
for the marriage of the Lamb has come,
and his bride has made herself ready;
to her it has been granted to be clothed with fine linen, bright
    and pure"—
for the fine linen is the righteous deeds of the saints.

And the angel said to me, "Write this: Blessed are those who
are invited to the marriage supper of the Lamb" (Rev. 19:6–9a).

This text is foundational for understanding marriage between Christians, for here we see John's vision of what God intends for the whole world. The "bride" of this passage is the church, and the garment she wears "is made from the fabric of witnessing to the lordship of God and the Lamb."[51] Both partners in a marriage, then, are included in the figure of the bride, and what is being described is the relationship between God and the church. At the "marriage supper of the Lamb" all peoples will celebrate their unity with God in a relationship that is eternal and eternally life-giving. The results of this relationship "will be staggering," says Brian Blount. "First, God will wipe away every tear from their eyes. The cause of tears—mourning, crying, pain, even death itself (20:14)—will be removed."[52] Those who marry, then, celebrate only in part the love of God in which they share; one day they will be fully embraced by it.

This is very good news. For no matter how faithful a couple is to the vows that they take, no one is able to keep them perfectly. Promises are broken, pain is inflicted, and partners do not always "outdo one another in showing honor." The gift, however, is that all of our failures—inside of marriage and out—will be washed away in life-giving water (Rev. 7:17). God will cover every hurt, every broken place, even every death with overwhelming grace. And so each marriage feast celebrated on earth anticipates that great wedding banquet we will one day enjoy, when all shall be well. Knowing this gives a large measure of grace to all of us who would make promises, for who among us—even those who enjoy long and happy marriages—can ever fully keep the vows we make? At a wedding between Christians, a couple with all of their guests participate in the foretaste of the eschatological banquet—the marriage supper of the Lamb—where every joy is complete and we are made one with God.

My friend Patrick Evans once recruited young talent for the school of music at Depauw University, and his job took him to high schools around the country. As he was making his way through the fine arts wing of one school, he heard what sounded like a voice teacher with a voice student, working on a popular-classical crossover tune. One voice was stronger but the other, though weaker, was still lovely, singing enthusiastically, if half a beat behind. Peeking through the window, Patrick saw a choral room with all of the furniture covered in plastic and one lone man painting the walls while singing along with whatever recording he had found on the teacher's desk. Those of us who marry are an awful lot like that tenor gamely singing along with a CD while he painted. Our offbeat, unskilled attempts at creating harmony in a marriage only hint at the beauty that is possible—and sometimes not even that. But even our amateurish marriages can be glorious in their own way, because we do get some things right, sometimes. And we keep at it, practicing the scales of true love, singing to the best of our ability, thankful for unexpected moments of transcendent joy and undeserved grace.

It must be said, of course, that one does not need to be married to see a glimpse of the coming reign of God. Nor does every marriage bring to mind heavenly bliss. Nevertheless, to live out a marriage with an eschatological view is to seek continually to grow in love while also accepting grace for ourselves and for our partners. This confidence in the promised realm to come means that each day we can renew our own promises and trust in the Spirit to increase in us kindness, patience, and the ability to forgive. This framework also informs the church on how to respond when vows are broken or marriages end. Even in this day and age when divorce is more widely accepted, the church often remains a place of silence, at best, or shame, at worst. We will consider divorce and remarriage more carefully in chapter 6; here we acknowledge that all marriages—those that last, and those that do not—involve failure and the need for grace.

THE PROMISES AND PRACTICES OF MARRIAGE

In chapter 3 we asked, along with Margaret Farley, whether marriage can bear the weight we have placed upon it. In one sense the answer is no, of course not. This is, in part, because we continue to promote, through popular songs and other forms of entertainment, what author Wendell Berry calls "the lure of sexual romance." The young "have been taught a series of extremely dangerous falsehoods," he writes:

1. That people in love ought to conform to the fashionable models of physical beauty, and that to be unbeautiful by these standards is to be unloveable.
2. That people in love are, or ought to be, young—even though love is said to last "forever."
3. That marriage is a solution—whereas the most misleading thing a love story can do is to end "happily" with a marriage, not because there is no such thing as a happy marriage, but because marriage cannot be happy except by being made happy.
4. That love, alone, regardless of circumstances, can make harmony and resolve serious differences.
5. That "love will find a way" and so finally triumph over any kind of practical difficulty.
6. That the "right" partners are "made for each other," or that "marriages are made in Heaven."
7. That lovers are "each other's all" or "all the world to each other."
8. That monogamous marriage is therefore logical and natural, and "forsaking all others" involves no difficulty.

By perpetuating such fallacies, insists Berry, we ensure that "a young couple could not be more cruelly exposed to the abrasions of experience."[53] Berry's stark identification of the lies we tell, often unknowingly, underscores the need for an eschatological framework for marriage. It is not only that such a perspective offers grace in the face of a failed marriage but that all marriages (like all people) are inherently flawed. When married people recognize, however, that their covenant involves tremendous challenges and that failing to live up to marriage vows is part and parcel of being married, then they are freed to forgive themselves and one another and empowered to rely on the sanctifying grace of Jesus Christ to continually strengthen and deepen their bonds. When we place our expectations of marriage within a larger eschatological framework, we discover that there is more to marriage than we imagined. It does not mean that we stop trying our very best to keep our vows, nor does it mean we give up on the possibility of a lifelong commitment. It does mean that we enter a marriage—and live out a marriage— in a covenant of grace, continually seeking to honor, uphold, serve, and delight in one another.

An eschatological framework for understanding marriage also dispels any illusions that this covenant is primarily for meetings one's personal needs. In one of Kathleen Norris's monastery sojourns, a monk explained that "'the basis of community is not that we all have our personal needs met here, or that we all find our best friends in the monastery.' In fact, he added, his pastoral experience with married couples had taught him that such unreasonably high expectations of any institution, be it a marriage or a monastery, was often what led to disillusionment, and dissolution of the bond." The monk went on to explain that both monks and married people must continually seek why they live together. "It's a common meaning," he said, "reinforced in the scriptures, a shared vision of the coming reign of God."[54]

Wendell Berry echoes something of the same sentiment

when he reflects that there are times in a marriage when we realize that "what we have chosen and what we desire are the same." This happens in a series of moments; it is not a permanent state. Yet fidelity, asserts Berry, "prepares us for the return of these moments, which give us the highest joy we can know; that of union, communion, atonement (in the root sense of at-one-ment)."[55]

In all of our relationships—and particularly in our marriages—we see glimpses of what is possible, we taste the promise of the life that is to come, and we trust in the constancy of the marriage bond even when (especially when) the days are difficult.

In our life with Christ, we come to the eucharistic table, where the taste of good bread and the aroma of sweet wine remind us of the heavenly wedding banquet that awaits us. In sharing a holy meal, we remember God's faithfulness to us since the beginning of time and anticipate future glory. We are renewed for the living of our days, nourished by Christ's own grace, revived by the Spirit to continue the walk of discipleship until that great day when Christ comes again. There is something eucharistic about marriage when we remember God's faithfulness to us and seek to live out that faithfulness to one another. When we show grace, we live out Christ's injunction to forgive one another as we have been forgiven. And in those sublime moments of true communion, when gratitude overwhelms, we do indeed catch a glimpse of the union with God and all creation we will one day enjoy, which is our deepest desire.

Margaret Farley names the goals of marriage as "embodied and inspirited union, companionship, communion, fruitfulness, caring and being cared for, opening to the world of others, and lives made sacred in faithfulness to one another and to God."[56] To live into those goals is to live into the promises inherent in marriage—both the promises we make to one another and the promise of union with God and all of creation when Christ comes again. To do so we must take on the practices of marriage: intentional and mutual self-giving; daily forgiving; outdoing one another in showing honor to the other; delighting in one another, body, mind, and soul. No one of us can live out these practices by our own power, and so we depend on the grace of Jesus Christ when we fail to do them; rely on the power of the Holy Spirit to sustain, uphold, and sanctify us as we continually live into the mystery of marriage; and trust the unbreakable covenant that God makes with us as we seek to live out our own covenants together. If it sounds like an awful lot of hard work, it is. If it sounds like serious business, it is. If it sounds impossible, well, it is. And yet all things are possible with the God who imbues our life with unexpected mercies and time after time surprises us with astonishing joy, abundant hope, and deep, deep love.

This way of talking about marriage is decidedly Christian, but it need not be for Christians only. As long as people continue to seek to be married in the church, the church must seek to share with people—whether committed Christians or religiously indifferent—a view of marriage that grows out of deep convictions about the love, grace, and faithfulness of God. In doing so, we will concern ourselves with best practices, not proscriptions. We will imagine all the varied ways that a marriage can be fruitful, whether it produces children or not. We will celebrate marriage liturgies that acknowledge the contours of contemporary lives. We will uphold fidelity and hope with all our hearts for partnerships that are committed and lifelong. Yet when covenants cannot hold, we will seek redemption and practice forgiveness, all the while acknowledging that every one of us lives by grace alone. We love because God first loved us; marriage, with all of its problems and pitfalls, is a life of practices and promises—indeed, a school for love.

Chapter 5

THE CHRISTIAN WEDDING

Was it something I said that bound me to you?

—*Wendell Berry,*
"The Country of Marriage"

What a crazy, impossible promise . . .

—*Martha Moore-Keish,*
"Marriage: A New Way of Life"

WHAT'S A WEDDING FOR?

No one needs the church to get married. Plenty of people wed without the insights of Scripture, the counsel of clergy, or the center aisle of an impressive sanctuary. Couples can easily be married anytime, anywhere, and without any talk of God. In fact, there are all sorts of ways to get married, and instant, free online ordination means that anyone can officiate at a wedding.

On the one hand, weddings look like they have for a long time, according to journalist Courtney E. Martin: "Two young lovers, dressed beautifully, take vows in front of their family and friends. Celebration ensues. Drinks flow. Sublimely bad intergenerational dancing commences." If one looks a little closer, though, "the scene is so thoroughly modern. The bride is pregnant and no one bats an eyelash."[1] So is the celebrant, who has been ordained for such occasions by the Universal Life Church, an online entity that ordains anyone, regardless of practices or creed.[2] Martin goes on to describe how she sees the landscape

of marriage among people with no particular religious affiliation or belief:

> The wedding ceremony has been thoroughly remade in the
> last decade by a generation of young people who don't identify
> with a particular religious tradition. We crave ritual, but can't
> abide by moralizing. We believe in the power of making prom-
> ises in front of beloved witnesses. We delight in the idea that—
> in a time of obsolescence and disconnection—a ceremony like
> this weaves us into the larger, ancient tapestry of our two fam-
> ilies. We obviously love a good party, but we don't want to be
> married by a relative stranger. . . . We can't look to previous
> generations for wisdom, as most of them were either married
> by a religious figure by choice or obliged by their parents.[3]

In one sense, it seems that this generation of lovers is looking for something entirely new. In another sense, however, what
they are seeking sounds an awful lot like what a Christian wedding ought to be like—a ritual event where people make promises in public, one that creates a community of love and support.

So what's a wedding for? At the most basic level, a wedding marks a significant transition in the lives of two people.
All weddings involve some sort of ritual—a way of marking
the event—saying vows, to be sure, and, often, giving rings.
Christian weddings include these things, too, but they are done
within the context of worship. Simply put, a Christian wedding
is a worship service. The faith of the church is proclaimed as
a couple makes promises in the midst of a community, people
who not only witness their joy and express their support but
also uphold them in prayer.

"So, this is what getting married is like," thought my
friend David Maxwell, in the middle of the wedding service
he thought would never take place. As a Presbyterian minister
he had presided at a number of weddings, but now he found
himself standing with his beloved partner of twenty-plus years,
making promises and receiving blessings. For a long time he
and Marcelo thought that they didn't need the institution of

marriage; their relationship had worked pretty well without it. But once state laws and denominational polities began to change, they decided to get married and, to David's surprise, it made a difference:

> Our relationship was taken out of the control of our private home and placed in front of friends and God. Everyone present prayed to God, asking for a blessing and for strength to honor promises made. We repeated vows used by millions of our ancestors in the faith. Both of our voices quivered as we looked through our tears at one another and promised things assumed for more than twenty years but never said in this way. Whatever bitterness or sarcasm my heart held toward marriage melted away.[4]

Despite protestations that marriage is "just a piece of paper" or that getting married doesn't change anything, something happens when two people stand in front of God and everybody and make promises. It makes a difference when a community gathers around those two people to say, by their very presence, that this bond matters and that they not only witness it but also uphold it with love and prayer. This public ceremony of commitment acknowledges, too, that the vows made by a couple affect a whole web of people and relationships. As such, a wedding marks the beginning of a life together, not the grand finale of a process that ends in marriage. Even for those who have lived together for a period of time, a wedding signals a new way of being in the world.

At an even deeper level, a Christian wedding is a way that a couple, in the midst of the community that surrounds them, acts out who they are trying to be but are not yet. Two people make vows, entering into what they assume will be a lifelong commitment of mutual love and care, speaking into being the sort of profound bond to which they aspire. A marriage liturgy, then, does not just define what marriage is—it evokes what it might be.[5]

At the heart of it all, however, is the worship of the triune God. A wedding is about the couple getting married, yes, but it is not only about the private relationship between two people, for their lives are related to so many others and, ultimately, to what God is doing in the world. The expressions of love and tears of joy happen in the context of prayers of thanksgiving, intercessions, and hymns of praise. The wedding of two people is one part of the large tapestry that is the story of God's love for them and for the whole world. Furthermore, everyone who gathers—families, friends, church members, musicians—has a part to play in bearing witness to the overwhelming love of God, proclaiming the promises of the gospel, expressing support for the marriage, and praying for the couple, those present, and the world—not only for the sake of the couple, but for the sake of all who gather to worship, and to the glory of God.

PASTORAL WISDOM

Clergy who preside at weddings must be theologically and pastorally nimble. A Christian marriage liturgy assumes that at least one of the partners is a baptized Christian, but in reality, all sorts of people come to be married. Some couples are from two different faiths, and others have no faith or are unsure about what they believe. In each case, pastors must balance sensitivity to the faith journeys of others with their role as Christian clergy; or, to put it another way, pastors need to be flexible and attentive to the needs of couples while also maintaining their theological integrity.

In the case of interfaith weddings, couples may choose to have two separate religious services. When both faiths are represented in one wedding service, it is crucial that the clergy from both faiths are involved in the planning. Prayers and other rituals are undertaken with an ethic of hospitality, and those attending the wedding are invited to participate as is appropriate for their own faith traditions. The goal is not to create a generic service that offends no one; rather, the idea is to shape a service that honors the religious traditions of both partners. The idea of "respectful presence" is helpful when considering how to conduct interfaith weddings. Those planning the wedding will incorporate elements from both faith traditions in a way that honors each. Neither tradition is dominant, and members of each faith tradition testify to their religious convictions and engage in authentic worship practices.[6]

ELEMENTS OF A MARRIAGE SERVICE

Any service of Christian worship can take place anywhere, and so it is with weddings. In discussing the marriage service, however, I will assume that the wedding is taking place in a sanctuary or other designated worship space, where the assembled community encounters the primary symbols of worship: the Bible, the baptismal font, and the Communion table. In the pages that follow, I will walk through the elements of a marriage liturgy, offering theological perspective and practical commentary. Although not all liturgies order the elements the same way, I will use the following pattern:

Gathering
Word
Vows
Prayer
Sacramental Acts
Charge and Blessing

Within this basic form is a great deal of freedom for couples to choose readings, vows, music, and so forth. When nuptials take place within the Sunday service, the couple move forward to make their vows after the reading and preaching of Scripture.

In other traditions, the vows precede the proclamation of the
Word.

Gathering

Entrance. There is no one way to get a wedding started. The traditional pattern of groom, attendants, and clergy waiting at the
front of the church while the bride and her attendants process
down the aisle is still alive and well. Alternatively, attendants
may come down the aisle together, or the couple being married
may process in accompanied by parents or other family members. Processions may happen to instrumental music or to the
singing of a congregational hymn. Or there might be no procession at all, but simply a gathering of those in the wedding party.
If the wedding takes place as part of Sunday morning worship,
members of the wedding party enter the sanctuary before the
service begins and take their seats near the front of the church.

It has become popular in some circles to use the entrance
of the bridal party as an opportunity to surprise and delight
the gathered congregation. A brief survey of YouTube.com
offers an astonishing array of production numbers performed
by attendants and couples entering the church to be married,
and even a rather exuberant Anglican vicar who takes center
stage in a flash-mob disco routine between the pronouncement
of marriage and the prayer of blessing. Don't do it. Save your
dancing for the reception—not because it isn't "religious" but
because entering a marriage is one of the most profound acts
in life and deserves to be marked with simple dignity and deep
gratitude to God.

Whatever method is used to enter the sanctuary, it is customary for the presider to face the congregation. When the two
being married are a woman and a man, traditionally the woman
stands to the presider's right. The couple face the presider until
it is time to speak their vows, when they turn to face each other.

Opening words. Many marriage liturgies begin with sentences of Scripture and/or a statement on the church's understanding of marriage. Marriage is often called a gift, created and given by God; some liturgies include an allusion to Ephesians 5:32, in which marriage is compared to the bond between Christ and the church. The opening statements that appear in many approved denominational liturgies allude to familiar passages of Scripture—the marriage canon described in chapter 4—in ways that perpetuate hierarchical and heteronormative models of marriage. Pastors and couples may want to give attention to those opening statements to find ways of making the language more inclusive and more reflective of the affirmations of marriage discussed in the previous chapter. The following example, grounded in Scripture, reflects an understanding of marriage as rooted in creation, shaped by the Christ event, and upheld by the Holy Spirit:

> Sisters and brothers,
> we are gathered here to celebrate the union of N. and N.,
> to witness the vows they make to one another,
> to pledge our support and encouragement,
> and to seek God's blessing upon their marriage.
>
> God created us for companionship
> and gave us the capacity for joy.
> Jesus Christ showed us self-giving love
> and taught us to continually forgive.
> And the Holy Spirit, given in our baptism,
> renews grace within us day by day
> and enables us to grow in faith, in hope, and in love.
>
> Marriage is a gift and a calling
> in which two people become for one another
> a source of love,
> a fount of blessing,
> and a deep well of grace,
> bearing each other's burdens
> and sharing in each other's joys.

As N. and N. commit their lives to one another,
families are joined,
friendships are forged and strengthened,
and a new community of love is formed.
As we bear witness to the vows being made today,
let us surround N. and N. with affection and prayer,
giving thanks for all the ways
that God's love is made manifest in their lives.[7]

Prayer. Here worshipers may thank God for marriage, acknowledge God's faithfulness, or ask for the Holy Spirit to enable the couple to keep the promises they will make, as in this prayer approved for use by the Episcopal Church:

Holy Trinity, one God,
three Persons perfect in unity and equal in majesty:
Draw together with bonds of love and affection
N. and *N.*, who with *their families*
seek to live in harmony and forbearance all their days,
that their joining together will be to us
a reflection of that perfect communion
which is your very essence and life,
O Father, Son, and Holy Spirit,
who live and reign in glory everlasting. *Amen.*[8]

A prayer of confession and declaration of forgiveness may also be included at this point in the service. All people fail to live as faithfully and love as well as God intends. Here, at the beginning of a service of marriage, a couple—and indeed, all who are present—can confess that they hurt one another even when they do not mean to, admitting their need for forgiveness. Such a prayer is followed by a strong proclamation of the grace of God, which heals every wound and covers every wrongdoing. After worshipers are called to confession with the promise of mercy, a congregation might pray the following:

Gracious God,
we confess that we do not always keep faith
with you or one another.

We tear down when we should build up;
we hurt one another when we mean to be kind;
we fail to forgive as you have forgiven us.
Have mercy on us, O God.

Soften our hearts,
enlarge our capacity to care,
and conform our wills to your own,
that we may love one another well
and serve you with joy.
In Jesus' name we pray.

A declaration of forgiveness that reminds the congregation of the baptismal covenant then follows:

Hear the good news!
[Water may be poured into the baptismal font.]
In the waters of baptism we are given new life,
freed from the sin that binds us,
and sent forth to reflect the light of Christ
to all we meet.
Sisters and brothers, believe the gospel!
In Jesus Christ, we are forgiven.[9]

Couples begin their marriage as forgiven people who, though they will inevitably hurt one another, are charged to forgive each other as Christ forgives them and are assured, from the very start, that God's grace is stronger than the damage they can do.

Declarations of intent. Here each partner affirms that she or he desires to enter into marriage. Replacing the betrothal rite found in some historic liturgies, this affirmation serves as a public acknowledgment that each person gives consent to the marriage and is entering into it by his or her own free will. While this might seem unnecessary in the twenty-first century, this element is retained to underscore that people are to enter marriage freely and without coercion.

In some cases, this is as simple as asking, "N., do you freely choose N. and intend to enter the covenant of marriage?"[10] In other cases, each partner is asked to affirm that she or he desires to live out the Christian vocation through marriage:

> N., in your baptism
> you have been called to union with Christ and the church.
> Do you intend to honor this calling
> through the covenant of marriage?[11]

This statement is intended to be brief and precedes the taking of marriage vows.

Affirmations of the families and the congregation. Also called "pledges of support" or "promises and blessings of families," this element takes the place of "giving away" the bride. Some independent and resourceful women still enjoy the tradition of being presented for marriage by a father or other male relative, reinterpreting the ritual gesture as sentimental in nature rather than economic. Some couples, however, choose to ask both families—and sometimes the entire gathered assembly as well—to pledge their support of the couple in their marriage. It can be a powerful moment when a couple hears all those gathered loudly affirm that they will, indeed, do everything in their power to uphold this marriage. Those attending the wedding are not just spectators but participants who make promises of their own. In one contemporary liturgy, the couple is presented by family or friends, and the presider asks questions of them:

> Presider: Who presents N. and N., as they seek the blessing of God and the Church on their love and life together?
>
> Presenters: We do.
>
> Presider: Will you love, respect, and pray for N. and N., and do all in your power to stand with them in the life they will share?
>
> Presenters: We will.[12]

This participatory role of the assembly can be expressed in a number of ways. One pastor described to me a wedding where the couple tied their rings to an old family Bible, which was then passed around the congregation during the ceremony. Every worshiper prayed over the rings before the couple gave them to one another. Certainly participating in prayer, singing, and the sacrament of Communion (see below) also underscore the congregation's participation in the wedding.

Word

Reading of Scripture. Having gathered, prayed, and expressed its intentions, the congregation listens to the Word of God in Scripture. As noted in chapter 4, few biblical passages speak directly about marriage as the egalitarian and mutually minded relationship that many contemporary Christians assume. And yet Scripture is a living Word that continues to speak into every time and place.

A couple and their pastor might choose a passage that focuses on the extravagant love of God as the source of human love, a text on living together in harmony and mutual forbearance, or a selection from the marriage canon, offering a fresh interpretation. (See appendix A for more on texts and preaching.) Anyone may read a passage of Scripture at a wedding— friend, family member, or clergy. Couples may want to include nonbiblical readings as well; there is nothing inherently wrong with this, as long as the readings are edifying, but they should not replace the reading of Scripture, since proclamation of the Word is a central element of worship.

Choosing Scripture readings can be dicey when working with couples who have little connection with a faith community. They may not be familiar with Scripture or willing to choose overly "churchy" passages. Perhaps this is why 1 Corinthians 13 is so popular; it does not mention God and only once refers to faith. After one pastor read this passage at a wedding, a guest said, "That was really beautiful. Did you write that yourself?"[13] Suggest passages to a couple, ask them to read them together at home, then talk about what they hear in them regarding the nature of God, the love they share, or their vision of marriage. This conversation can be rich, opening doors to future inquiries about Christian faith.

Preaching. Many ministers say that they do not preach at weddings because no one is listening anyway. I used to be one of them. But I have come to understand how important preaching can be at a wedding. This is not an opportunity for a wise pastor to dispense sage advice to the couple, but it is a moment for proclaiming the radical love of God who created us for companionship, taught us to love as we have been loved, and empowers us with the divine Spirit so that we may care for others with a strength that goes far beyond our own. A wedding sermon speaks to everyone present, not only to the couple, in a manner that is broadly inclusive and acknowledges all the varied ways that grace is bestowed, so that blessing falls on the single and the divorced, the happily married, the lonely, and the lovelorn.

Preaching at a wedding is also an opportunity for sharing the good news of the gospel. By describing marriage within a Christian framework, preachers have a chance to name grace where they see it, pointing to ways that God is already at work in the lives of the two being married and in the wider world. A wedding sermon also ties the story of a couple to the greater story of God and God's people, bearing witness to the love of God that is the source of all human love. A preacher may describe the self-giving love of Jesus Christ as a model for the kind of mutual self-giving that happens, ideally, in all relationships and especially in marriage. Or one might preach on the work of the Holy Spirit who enables us to love more powerfully and live more faithfully than we could ever manage to do on our own.

In crafting a wedding sermon, a preacher might draw on the lives of the couple being married—their personal histories, their identity as Christians, their cultures, the story of their relationship. For Christians, a marriage is the joining of two people whose identity is in Jesus Christ, and the wedding sermon may reflect on their shared baptismal vocation, how their life together might reflect the love of Christ, or how their marriage might anticipate the coming reign of God.[14]

Vows

Exchange of vows. Making vows is the centerpiece of the wedding. No other words are as important, and no other ritual act should overshadow that of a couple facing one another, joining hands, and making promises before God and the gathered assembly. Even though life is uncertain and human beings are fickle creatures, the vows they make are unequivocal, expressing hope in the future and the sort of bond to which they aspire. To make a vow to another is to acknowledge, right from the start, that life together will be difficult as well as joyful, and to choose that life on the wedding day and every day thereafter. Taking such a vow is more than making a promise to oneself; it is a radical and countercultural giving of oneself to another— placing a part of oneself into the other's "keeping" so that each has a claim over the other.[15] Kathleen Norris underscores this radical nature of marriage vows when she says, "The very nature of marriage means saying yes before you know what it will cost. Though you may say the 'I do' of the wedding ritual in all sincerity, it is the testing of that vow over time that makes you married."[16]

The profound depth of marriage vows is, of course, all tied up in the mundane details of daily living. Such promises "spell out a rhythm of dying and rising," says Roman Catholic theologian Kathleen Hughes, "better and worse, sickness and health, poverty and riches." These familiar phrases are "metaphors for the rhythm of our days, of dishes and work schedules and children to be fed and cars that need servicing and the thousand details of life, large and small, that constitute the keeping of these promises—to say nothing of the crises, the moments of grief and loss, grave illness, financial woes, that form larger challenges to promise keeping."[17]

How can we make such vows, knowing that we will hurt one another and break promises? We make them in the belief that God is present not just on the wedding day but on every day to follow, and that by God's grace, all of our actions, including our failures, "will point to the faithfulness of God, who never fails."[18] This means that marriage vows echo the whole rest of the life of faith. We live into promises we cannot keep on our own; we lean into and rely upon the grace of God to enable us to show love and mercy.

In an inclusive marriage service that highlights the mutuality of the relationship, it is important that the vows use the same language for both partners. The minister may vary the order in which the partners make vows—that is, one partner may speak first during the marriage vows, and another speak first during the exchange of rings. In any case, it is not the minister who does the marrying; the two who make promises to one another constitute the marriage to which they commit themselves.

Sometimes a couple bring to their marriage children of their own union or from previous relationships. In some cases, but certainly not all, it is fitting to include the children in the making of vows. The couple may make promises to love and honor the children, publicly affirming a long-standing commitment or signaling the forming of a new kind of family. Children must never be coerced into taking part in a wedding ceremony, however, nor should they be required to make vows. For many couples, including the children in the affirmation of the families is a way to allow them to give voice to their support of the marriage (or not) without putting them in the spotlight or requiring them to say more than they wish.[19]

Exchange of rings. As seen in chapter 3, exchanging gifts has long been a part of wedding ceremonies. In recent times it is common for both partners to give rings to their mates. This ritual act serves as a visible confirmation of the central act of the wedding, the making of vows. The minister may say a prayer of blessing over the rings before giving them to the couple. If the couple being married has been in a committed relationship for an extended period of time and has been wearing rings exchanged long ago, this may be acknowledged in a prayer such as the following:

> By the rings which they have worn, faithful God,
> N. and N. have shown to one another and the world
> their love and faithfulness.
> Bless now these rings,
> that from this day forward
> they may be signs of the vows N. and N. have exchanged
> in your presence and in the communion of your Church,
> through Christ our Lord. *Amen.*[20]

Rituals common in various cultures, such as the giving of food, coins, or other gifts, may also be included here. In some Hispanic and Filipino communities, couples may include the blessing and giving of the *arras* (literally, "pledge"). In exchanging the *arras*—usually a small box or other vessel containing thirteen coins—the couple promise to share with one another all of the material goods that will come to them during their marriage. Others, especially Roman Catholic couples from Latin America, may incorporate the *lazo*, or lasso, a large rosary in the shape of a figure eight that is placed around their shoulders. The *lazo* signifies that they are bound together for the rest of their lives as they encounter joys and sorrows and support one another through mutual love and sacrifice.

African American couples sometimes include the tradition of "jumping the broom," a custom thought to have originated in Africa. Those considering incorporating this ritual may want to research the topic before making a decision. A number of scholars argue that this practice does not originate in Africa, as is widely believed, but with white plantation owners who required enslaved people to participate in it as a way of asserting their control and belittling the couple being married.[21]

Prayer

One of the great blessings of getting married in the midst of a Christian community is the opportunity for prayer. The worshiping body asks for God's blessing upon the couple and their life together, prays for those in the gathered assembly, and lifts up the needs of the world. It may seem odd to include such an expansive prayer at a wedding, where the focus is on two people—and that is precisely the point. A wedding is about the joining of two people in a lifelong commitment, yes, but it is also about the generativity of that commitment. A marriage affects far more than the two people involved, for a new network of people is formed. Furthermore, when Christians marry, the focus is not only on the love between them but also on their love for God and God's world. The inward-outward turn of married love discussed in chapter 4 is expressed in prayer at a wedding.

The prayer begins with supplication for the couple. In this prayer from the *Book of Common Worship*, one can hear this inward-outward turn:

> Give them wisdom and devotion in their common life,
> that each may be to the other
> a strength in need,
> a counselor in perplexity,

a comfort in sorrow,
and a companion in joy.

Grant that their wills may be so knit together in your will,
and their spirits in your Spirit,
that they may grow in love and peace
with you and each other
all the days of their life.

Give them the grace,
when they hurt each other,
to recognize and confess their fault,
and to seek each other's forgiveness
and yours.

Make their life together
a sign of Christ's love to this sinful and broken world,
that unity may overcome estrangement,
forgiveness heal guilt,
and joy conquer despair.

Give them such fulfillment of their mutual love
that they may reach out in concern for others.[22]

In this prayer, the congregation prays for the couple's life together, for growth in their relationship with God and one another, and for their witness and service to others. The prayer goes on to lift up the gathered community, that all may be strengthened in their lives and be a sign of the coming reign of God. Finally, the gathered assembly prays for the world:

Grant that the bonds by which all your children
are united to one another
may be so transformed by your Spirit
that your peace and justice may fill the earth,
through Jesus Christ our Lord.

Immediately after taking their vows, then, the couple is surrounded by prayer for their marriage, for their family and friends, and for the transforming love of God at work in the world.

Many wedding prayers mention the possibility of future children, praying for the couple's wisdom as parents. Pastors should carefully consider with a couple whether this portion of the prayer should be included. Some couples may not plan on raising children or may be beyond the age of bearing or nurturing offspring.

Western churches might take a page from their Eastern counterparts in praying for the Holy Spirit to infuse a marriage. While some Western marriage rites include a reference to the Holy Spirit, the most overt instance of calling on the Spirit is found in marriage liturgies of the Eastern Orthodox tradition. During a part of the liturgy called a crowning ceremony, the priest places crowns or garlands on the heads of the couple being married, marking the moment when the Spirit is invoked (the *epiclesis*).[23] Orthodox theologian Paul Evdokimov says this moment is "the time of the nuptial Pentecost, the descent of the Holy Spirit making a new creation."[24] The priest calls on the Spirit, praying, "O Lord our God, crown them with glory and honor." Anticipating the glory that will be theirs in the end time, the priest and all who join the prayer summon the Spirit to be at work in the meantime.[25] The marriage blessing found in *Evangelical Lutheran Worship* includes this petition: "By the power of your Holy Spirit pour out the abundance of your blessing upon *name* and *name*. Defend them from every enemy. Lead them into all peace. Let your love be a seal upon their hearts, a mantle about their shoulders, and a crown upon their foreheads." The prayer continues with a petition that "their lives together may bear witness to your love."[26]

A matrimonial epiclesis strikes me as a crucial element of a Christian wedding prayer. In every endeavor of the Christian life, it is the power of the Holy Spirit that enables us to pray to the triune God, serve Jesus Christ, and continually grow in faith. Christians who marry might well affirm that it is the Spirit who allows them to love ever more deeply, live in fidelity, and show hospitality as a couple. Roman Catholic author Julie McCarty describes the Holy Spirit as the "bonding agent" of the church that "penetrates and permeates the persons being gathered" into the one body of Christ, a communion of persons. So, too, she argues, does the Spirit bond two people in marriage, not only on their wedding day but throughout their marriage.[27] In praying for a couple in this expansive way, a congregation might also lay hands on them during such a prayer—or stretch their hands toward the couple in a gesture of blessing—enacting their role as the body of Christ in upholding two people as they pledge to share their lives with one another.

Sacramental Acts

Baptismal symbols. In marriage, two people live out their baptismal vocation, in part, through their life together. It is fitting, then, that baptismal language and symbolism appear in the wedding service. Sometimes an enthusiastic wedding coordinator will rush to move a baptismal font or Communion table "out of the way" so that the bridal party can pass freely through the worship space. Yet encountering the font during a wedding might actually be a source of blessing. Imagine a couple moving toward the front of the sanctuary and passing their hands through a centrally located font on their way to making vows. A couple may also reaffirm their baptism at the beginning of the service, in connection with the declaration of intent. This might be done with a brief liturgy, such as the following:

Pastor: [*Names*], years ago, your parents brought you into
a place like this and presented you for Christian

baptism. At that time you received the sign and seal of God's steadfast love and were welcomed into God's kingdom. God put his hand on you and called you to be in union with Christ, his Son and his body, the church. Since that day, you have made your profession of faith in Jesus Christ and have sought to serve him as your Savior and Lord.

Today is a bright new day for you. But first we are called back to that long-ago day of your baptism that affects this one mightily. That day God welcomed you into the covenant community. That day you came under the sign of Christ's death and resurrection, of dying daily to sin, and rising each day to live the covenant life of righteousness and thankful obedience. Today I ask you, Do you affirm your baptism, do you affirm your faith in Jesus Christ, and do you intend to honor your calling as a child of God and as a member of his body through the covenant of marriage you make today?

Couple: I do. I remember my baptism and I here make covenant to live my baptism daily.

[*The couple may dip their fingers or hands in the water and touch their own or each others' heads. This should be done without words. But use pastoral discretion; avoid the impression that this is a re-baptism.*][28]

A couple may underscore their understanding of marriage as part of a Christian vocation by being anointed with oil, which is a repeatable part of the baptismal rite. This might happen as part of the declaration of intent or as part of the prayers; the couple may be anointed by the presider, or each partner may anoint the other, perhaps by making a sign of the cross on the forehead. The accompanying language should be simple, calling the couple to remember their baptism and be thankful.

Eucharist. From the wedding at Cana (John 2) to the marriage supper of the Lamb (Rev. 19), eucharistic imagery is tied to marriage. The Communion table is the place where Christ invites us to union with him and with one another. It is the place of reconciliation, and the meal we share is a foretaste of the heavenly banquet we shall one day share. Consider how the first part of one eucharistic prayer written for use at weddings picks up various biblical references to marriage:

> Holy mystery,
> energy that powers the universe,
> your Word set creation into motion:
> ever-expanding, evolving, multiplying, flourishing.
> You brought human life out of primordial mist,
> setting us in this garden home,
> instilling in us the capacity to love,
> endowing us with the imagination
> to form friendships and make love.
> We heard you tell our ancient parents
> that it is not good to be alone
> and command them to fill the earth with blessing.
> Yet, so often, we were afraid.
> We failed to nurture your good creation.
> We limited the wideness of your love
> by pretending that some are loved by you,
> and others are outside your grace.
> Again and again, you sent men to remind us of mercy,
> and women to demand justice.
> At the right time, you sent Jesus,
> an open channel of light and love,
> who turned water into wine,
> rejection into welcome,
> hunger into fullness,
> and death into life.[29]

This prayer after Communion expresses well the rich symbolism of the Table with regard to union with Christ and one another, particularly in light of marriage:

> Faithful, loving God,
> we give you thanks
> that you have made us one flesh, one people
> in the body and blood of our beloved Savior.
> Those whom you have joined together,
> let no one separate.
>
> Now make us ready for that banquet to come
> at the wedding feast of the Lamb
> and the marriage of heaven and earth,
> when all will be holy and all will be whole.
> Until that great day keep us loving and faithful,
> praying maranatha—come, Lord Jesus, come. *Amen.*[30]

Couples and pastors must think carefully about whether Communion ought to be celebrated at a wedding. Certainly if the gathered congregation is primarily Christian, there would be few compelling reasons not to include the sacrament. If, however, a great number of guests would not be able to participate, a couple must decide whether it is more hospitable to include the sacrament or to refrain from doing so. When Eucharist is celebrated, it is important that the bread and wine be offered to all Christians, not just the couple, since by nature it is a communal meal. A couple might consider taking part in serving the bread and wine as their first act of marriage, if church polity allows it. Some denominations require that the reading of Scripture and preaching of a sermon must accompany the celebration of Communion.

Footwashing. Footwashing is most commonly practiced as part of worship on Holy (or Maundy) Thursday, but it can also be done at weddings. Although vow-making remains the central act of the service, partners may wash one another's feet as a sign of their mutual love and care for one another as well as an expression of their servanthood to Jesus Christ. The footwashing may be extended to include in-laws (that is, one partner washes the feet of the other's parents) and, indeed, the whole congregation, if desired. It is not necessary to add a great many spoken words; the act communicates well enough.

Charge and Blessing

Announcement of marriage. Although it is not necessary to include an announcement of marriage, it is common for a presider to pronounce the couple married either after vows are made and any other ritual acts take place or after the vows and before a prayer of blessing. Since it is not the minister who marries the couple but the partners themselves, any announcement refers to the couple's own vows. Although some couples may choose to use the traditional language of husband and wife, it is also possible to announce the marriage in a more inclusive way:

> N. and N. have made promises to one another
> in the presence of God and this assembly
> and have sealed those promises with the giving and receiving
>   of rings.
> Let their marriage be held in honor by all.[31]

If the couple bring children to their union, the following words might be said:

> By the vows made this day
> in the presence of God and this community,
> I declare that N. and N.
> are now joined in the covenant of marriage.
> In the household of faith,
> we rejoice with them and their children
> on this glad occasion,
> and celebrate with joy their life together.[32]

Announcing the marriage this way makes it unnecessary for the minister to "present" the couple to the congregation as Mr. and Mrs. So-and-So.

Charge to the couple. The epistles offer fitting language with which to charge a couple. It is hard to improve on this passage from Colossians 3, for example:

> As God's own,
> clothe yourselves with compassion,
> kindness, and patience,
> forgiving each other
> as the Lord has forgiven you,
> and crown all these things with love,
> which binds everything together in perfect harmony.[33]

More meaningful than any clever joke or nugget of advice that might be spoken at this time, these words evoke a vision of marriage that is blessed and nourished by Christ's own love.

Blessing of the congregation. A charge may be addressed to the couple, but a benediction is spoken to the entire congregation, just as in any service of worship.

Kiss. As discussed in chapter 3, the wedding kiss originated with the kiss of peace. A presider may replace the traditional "you may kiss the bride" with the more egalitarian "you may now share a kiss" or "the peace of Christ be with you." Or simply let the kissing commence with no words at all.

PRACTICAL MATTERS

Music at weddings. The music played and sung at weddings functions the same way it does in any worship service. There may be hymns of praise, songs of thanksgiving, or sung prayers of supplication from a wide range of musical styles. What is important is that wedding music is offered for the glory of God and reflects the faith of the church. Pastors and church musicians are full of stories about couples wanting popular love songs sung at their wedding; these decisions may be the arena where there is the least amount of understanding between clergy and musicians, on one hand, and couples who want to marry, especially those with little or no experience with the Christian faith. Generally speaking, songs expressing romantic love are most appropriately sung at the reception, as they place the focus on the intimate relationship between the two who are marrying rather than on God, who is the source of all love. Although ministers are the final arbiters of these decisions, the wisest ones help couples understand the role of music in a service of worship and steer them toward music that, at the very least, does not conflict with Christian faith and practice.

So what does that music sound like? It may sound like one acoustic guitar or an organ, a string quartet or a gospel choir. Certainly there is a place for instrumental music and solo singing, but congregational singing allows the gathered assembly to participate even more fully in a wedding. (See appendix B for a list of hymns and songs especially suitable for a Christian wedding.)

Working through questions of music can be especially thorny with couples who view the church—or any space made sacred by worship—as a venue rather than a place where the worshiping community gathers. Pastors who are clear that their wedding ministry is tied to their identity as a Christian minister, and not as a functionary of the state or a vendor of wedding services, will allow their vocation to guide them. At its best, the music sung and played at a wedding points to the glory of God, whatever the style might be. Yet there may be times when pastoral wisdom leads one to agree that a romantic ballad or sentimental song might be exactly the right thing. This may sound heretical to some of my pastoral and musical colleagues, but I have learned that it is best to avoid fundamentalism of any type!

So how do a couple and their pastor choose music for a wedding? It is helpful to think of function first—that is, what does music do? Songs and hymns can proclaim Scripture; they can help worshipers respond to Scripture or voice prayers. A congregation might sing "Joyful, Joyful We Adore Thee" as a wedding processional or first hymn, to give praise to the One who is "God of glory, Lord of love." A couple who see their marriage as part of living out their Christian vocation might choose to seal their vows by singing with the congregation "Take My Life and Let It Be Consecrated" or "Called as Partners in Christ's Service." Singing "Love Divine, All Loves Excelling" reminds all those at a wedding that Christ gives us his own compassion, the Spirit sets us free to go forth in faith, God is perfect love, and we will one day all be "lost in wonder, love, and praise." Not a bad way to start a life together.

Several contemporary hymn writers have penned texts specifically for weddings. Herman Stuempfle's "Unseen God, Your Hand Has Guided" acknowledges God's role in bringing together two people in marriage and prays for their marriage.[34] Mary Louise Bringle's hymn "Love Has Brought Us Here Together" draws on biblical texts from the Song of Songs and 1 Corinthians 13.[35] "Rejoice in Christ the Lord! (In Love Abide)" by David Gambrell draws on the vine-and-branches imagery of John 15, and Michael Morgan's "A Hymn in Praise of God's Love" extols the love of God that is the source of all human love and seals promises made between two people in marriage.[36] A number of hymnals include a section on weddings in the topical index. A comprehensive list of appropriate hymns, choral anthems, vocal solos, organ selections, and works for instrumental ensembles is available from the Presbyterian Association of Musicians.[37]

Can popular songs be appropriate for a wedding? In some

cases, the answer is yes, but they are most often best sung by a soloist, since the rhythms and vocal techniques of pop music are intended to be sung by one voice (or with harmony or backup voices). The 1997 hit song "All My Life" by K-Ci & JoJo is beautiful and heartfelt; the singer says he has prayed for the one he loves and thanks God for bringing them together. Yet the focus is primarily on the love between two people rather than the providence of God, which would cause some pastors and church musicians to deny a request for this song. For some couples who are still seeking a spiritual path, however, this may be the closest they can get to naming the possibility that God plays a part in their life together. That said, it could only be sung effectively by a skilled duo with a talented ensemble.

At the heart of the question is this: Should music for a wedding focus on the love of God and the faith of the church or on the love story of the couple who is marrying? As a service of worship, a Christian wedding demands that God remains central to the proceedings, and that pertains to the music that is sung. At the same time, a wedding—like a funeral—tethers the story of a couple to the larger story of God and God's people. Particularity is important; it matters *who* is getting married, just as it matters who is being buried. For that reason, there should be some stretching and bending when it comes to music for a wedding. Does that mean pastors and musicians are forced to make judgment calls sometimes? Yes, it does. Sometimes the integrity of the service is maintained by saying no to a couple's request. Other times, the overwhelming grace of God covers the quirks and foibles of lovesick human beings, and a pastor or musician may say yes to a questionable song because the reasons for doing so are more important than the reasons for not. If I have exquisite musical taste, flawless liturgical theology, and unquestionable good judgment, but have not love . . .

Nevertheless, it is useful to have theological principles in place from which one might occasionally deviate. In general, music at weddings gives thanks to God, proclaims God's glory, and prays for the abiding power of love. Such music takes a couple and those worshiping with them beyond the realm of their personal relationship and into the very realm of God, who intends love and justice for all God's people.

Photography. An astute pastor will make sure that the couple has communicated to any photographers or videographers that the wedding is a service of worship. For many churches, this means that flash photography is prohibited during the ceremony. Insist that photographers and videographers practice their craft discreetly, not roaming around obtrusively or popping up at unexpected moments. A note in a printed order of worship, or a sign near the entrance to the sanctuary, can request that guests refrain from taking photographs during the wedding. A cordial greeting and request before the ceremony can also help ensure that photographers and videographers respect the holy ground on which they walk.

Wedding coordinators. Wedding planning has become big business, and wedding coordinators are often on the scene the day of the service. Some are well acquainted with common practices of Christian weddings; others are not. Wedding coordinators can be quite helpful with the logistics of processions, seating of family members, and so forth. A pastor, however, is the final authority when it comes to the marriage liturgy. Families can affirm their support for a marriage; a bride does not have to be given away. The font, table, or pulpit do not need to be moved for expediency's sake or to accommodate the last-minute flourishes of an enthusiastic florist. A wedding is a service of worship, and if it takes place in a sanctuary, the liturgical furniture is a part of how the space communicates what God is doing in the church and in the world.

Wedding policies. A church's wedding policy ensures that pastors and musicians do not have to make judgment calls every time another wedding comes around. Furthermore, they allow the church to understand weddings as part of their mission (more on this in chap. 6) and give church leaders the opportunity to thoughtfully consider the theological issues at hand. Wedding policies also allow churches to be intentional about the stewardship of their property as well as the time and energy of their pastors. A church's wedding policy must, of course, be in concert with the polity of the denomination.

Questions to be addressed in a marriage policy include the following items:

Must the bride and groom both be church members? Must they both be Christians?

How far in advance of the wedding must a request be made? Who approves requests?

When may weddings take place? Are there particular times during the church year—such as Holy Week, Easter, or the seasons of Advent or Lent—when weddings may not be held?

Must the wedding take place in the church's sanctuary? If not, what other settings, on or off church property, are approved?

May Christians from other congregations—or people from other faiths—hold weddings in the church's sanctuary?

May clergy from other churches or faiths conduct weddings in the church? May civil authorities preside at weddings in the church?

What parts of the church's building and grounds may be used? Are there restrictions on decorations, the use of nails or tacks or tape, or the throwing of birdseed, confetti, or rice?

May the church's liturgical furniture—such as pulpit, table, and font—be moved?

What guidelines apply to photographers, videographers, and guests?

May alcohol be served on church property?

Who approves musical selections, and what criteria are used?

May guest musicians be involved? May prerecorded music be used?

What is fair compensation for church musicians? (Please consult with musicians on this point; many belong to organizations with their own professional guidelines.)

Will the church charge fees for use of the building or grounds, custodial service, or sound technicians? If so, are church members exempt from these fees?

Is there a suggested or required honorarium for the pastor?

Does the church need a person or group to serve as a coordinator or liaison to work with couples and help them follow the guidelines?

Is the pastor required to counsel couples prior to their marriage? (Some denominations require this.) If so, how often? May the pastor refer couples to other counselors?[38]

Wedding rehearsals. Even with the simplest weddings, it is useful to have some sort of rehearsal. When many people are involved, it is essential! A wedding, like any worship service, is something of a drama—God is glorified when we are prepared, know our roles, and can enter fully into the worship of God, prayer, and the making of promises.

There is no one right way, of course, to conduct a wedding rehearsal, but a few suggestions can help things run smoothly. While not all churches require musicians to be present for a rehearsal, it is often helpful for all involved to hear musical cues and have a sense of the mood and pace of the hymns, songs, or instrumental pieces. New pastors do well to humbly invite the musicians of the churches to attend those first rehearsals; often the musicians are far more familiar with the mechanics of weddings than anyone!

Excitement is high, nerves are on edge, and anxiety is raging at most wedding rehearsals. Family dynamics—positive and negative—are just below the surface. Power plays and rivalries can emerge. Children can be rolling under pews or racing down aisles. It falls to the pastor to be a calming and gentle, but firm, presence.

Gather everyone involved in the wedding in the front pews or chairs, and ask family members to be seated where they will be during the wedding. Introduce yourself, welcome everyone, and open with prayer. Explain that you will be going through the entire service at least once and then ask the wedding party to take their places.

Begin the rehearsal with everyone in place—any processions are rehearsed later. Talk through the service, giving instructions and explanations as warranted. Ask the two people marrying to say their vows aloud and practice exchanging rings (even if pantomiming). Explain what follows and how the service will end. Be sure everyone knows who is responsible for the rings on the day of the wedding. You might even designate an attendant to retrieve a dropped ring to avoid unnecessary scrambling and bumping of heads!

Once you have gone through the service once, ask the wedding party to go to wherever they will be before entering the worship space. Rehearse any processions or entries until everyone seems comfortable with the procedure. If young children are involved, be sure that a trusted adult accompanies them, and always have a plan B! Kids react differently to public situations; some love the attention while others flee the spotlight. If it is warranted, go through the entire service again. Otherwise, proceed to rehearsing how the wedding party will leave the worship space.

If there are hymns to be sung, be sure there are hymnbooks or copies available. Rehearse the hymns so that the wedding party is familiar with them and can take part fully.

If there will be a sermon or Communion, be sure to include instructions for where and how the wedding party will be seated.

When all the details have been covered, close the rehearsal with prayer and dismiss the wedding party with thanks.[39]

Chapter 6

MARRIAGE AND THE CHURCH'S MISSION

When churches consider their mission, they rarely name marriage among their goals. To be sure, pastors and congregations play a large role in the lives of couples before, during, and after a wedding. Yet marriage can be woven into the ongoing life and mission of the church, as Christians deepen their understanding of marriage as part of their baptismal vocation and affirm the sacred worth of all people. The church can also be a place of healing and redemption for people experiencing divorce, through ongoing teaching, pastoral care, congregational support, and, in some cases, liturgy.

BEFORE THE WEDDING

Pastors have long considered premarital counseling an important part of their ministry, and, indeed, some denominations require this counseling of their clergy. Many rely on instruments that require them to administer inventories, interpret them, and teach relationship skills, and these can be useful tools. Yet the church has a particular ministry, helping couples think about marriage theologically, biblically, and spiritually. A variety of professionals can administer inventories, but only the church speaks about the deep mystery of Christ's grace and the love of God that is the source of all human love. Do the inventories, yes, but do not stop there.

Talking through the elements of a marriage service enables pastors and couples to consider together the nature of love, the role of forgiveness, and the need for the work of the Spirit. Discussing the wedding liturgy can help couples understand their marriage as both public and personal, and it offers an opportunity to talk about family dynamics that might be at work, not only on the day of the wedding but in the months and years to come. Conversations around wedding plans can also allow couples to discuss their attitudes regarding money, parents, children, and past relationships.

Exploring the worship space with a couple also provides opportunities to share the church's story—both the gospel story and that of the local congregation—and to draw connections with their own story. When walking through the doors of the church, a pastor might note that people pass through those same doors during all sorts of life transitions. People come through the church doors to be baptized and welcomed into the body of Christ. They enter to celebrate great joys and to mourn deep sorrows. They come to hear words of comfort and challenge and to be strengthened for the living of their days. And when their earthly life is done, friends welcome their bodies at these doors to remember and to give thanks. A couple might then imagine themselves walking through those doors on the day of their wedding and know that others who have walked through those doors will be there to support them as they begin their marriage.[1]

Similarly, a minister might pause at the font, explaining that it is where Christians are given new life and joined to a community, perhaps sharing the story of a baptism that was particularly moving. At the Communion table, a pastor can explain that this is the place where the community gathers for a meal, just as families and friends gather around a table to be nourished and enjoy one another's company. At this table, Christ himself invites us, meets us, and gives us bread in order to strengthen us for the journey ahead.[2]

When couples sit down to plan a wedding that will take place in a sanctuary, they may be more apt to see it as a place that is significant to the lives of many people and not simply an attractive venue. Couples in which one or both partners are Christian, especially those who worship in that place, may deepen their understanding of how the space itself contributes to the meaning of their wedding.

Churches and their pastors take a variety of approaches in preparing couples for marriage. A pastor stresses to young couples that marriage is one of the biggest business decisions they will make in their lifetimes. Throwing the kind of wedding pictured in popular magazines and on slick Web sites is not an option for people in his rural, economically depressed community, so this pastor counsels couples to choose their mates wisely, considering whether they are likely to be able to keep a job or help support a family. He also talks with couples about how they will make their home a place of hospitality.

Some churches incorporate liturgical markers along the way as couples prepare for marriage. One pastor suggested asking couples to come to worship twice before the wedding; on the second time they would be acknowledged and the assembly would pray for them. In this way, the congregation would have a connection to what is going on in their building on a Saturday, and the couple would, at least in some small way, sense that there is a faith community who cares about them and their life together. That same couple might also come back to church when they return from the honeymoon and stand together in front of the congregation to be prayed for once again, perhaps with the laying on of hands by people who know them. "Just coming to the church for your wedding is not enough," the minister insisted. "That's not the church. That's a hall and a hired pastor." Will some couples look askance when the minister says the church wants them to come so they can pray for them? Maybe. But it could also come as a welcome surprise, this startling offer of care from strangers. With this simple act, a congregation takes a measure of responsibility for couples who will marry in their sanctuary and witnesses to the love of Jesus Christ.

Some churches require couples to attend church regularly before their wedding. In one case, couples were expected to come to church twice a month during their engagement—usually a span of about a year. By the time the wedding came around, the couples had been in worship fairly regularly, and a number of them even joined the church. Reflecting on the practice, the pastor of that church now wishes he had asked couples to return to the church on a Sunday morning one month after the wedding, so that the community could recognize them, pray for them, and promise to support them in their marriage.

DURING THE WEDDING

Since all faithful worship participates in the mission of God, weddings are, by definition, missional. In worship we declare the gospel, and at the heart of this gospel is a vision of life imbued with a holy love. Words of welcome point to the God who is the source of all love, the one who created us for companionship and mutual support. Affirmations of families exhibit the equality of the partners who marry, visibly and audibly showing that a new community of love is being formed by the union of two people. Through reading and preaching from Scripture, the church proclaims life-giving ways of living together. Through our prayers, we insist that a couple does not enter the country of marriage alone but accompanied by God, who will continually uphold and strengthen them, and by a whole cloud of witnesses, who pledge their support.

Furthermore, weddings call forth from a couple their intentions to live as disciples—in the world and also in their home. Two people can serve as disciples of Christ together, showing hospitality, feeding the hungry, giving comfort to those who suffer, as individuals and as a couple, depending on their particular gifts and graces. They can also live out that discipleship in their homes as they break bread at one table, forgive one another as God has forgiven them, and give each other comfort and care in the midst of sorrow or sickness.[3] By the power of the Holy Spirit, two people can not only sustain one another but also make each other better people, better disciples, better partners.

Meanwhile, the church is gathered around these two hopeful people who make ridiculous promises to each other, promises they can never fully keep but pledge to live into. What would happen if we asked our church leaders to show up for weddings as they do for funerals, to witness to the love and mercy of the triune God and pray for a couple's life together? It would not add to the expense of the wedding, for they would not attend the reception, unless it was one that the church provided.

I realize that my optimism is showing. I want the church to give this all away—the vision of love, the counsel, the prayers— without any thought of whether a couple become church members. Give it away with abandon—but give something that only Christians can offer, more than simply a pretty space and a competent officiant.

Among the gifts Christians offer is hospitality. Our marriage rites must reflect God's all-encompassing love and, therefore, be fully inclusive. While it is certainly acceptable to use language of husband and wife or male and female, many churches are turning to more inclusive wedding services that use nongendered language or offer options for the way a couple is named. Rather than offering one wedding service for gay folks and another one for straight people, use one inclusive marriage rite that holds all people equally beloved in the sight of God. More and more straight couples are asking for such language because of their own convictions or because friends or family members are gay, lesbian, or transgender. Furthermore, it is the mission of the church to bless those relationships that have flourished for years, in the midst of our own congregations and beyond, now that marriage equality is the law of the land.

We adopt inclusive marriage rites not only for the sake of stating our convictions, though. Using nongendered language signals to the closeted teen that he or she is welcome. It gives courage to the middle-aged father struggling with whether to meet his daughter's girlfriend and comfort to the mother who is afraid to let her church friends know that her son is gay. In doing so, we express our oneness in Christ and the love of God for all people.

AFTER THE WEDDING: THE ONGOING MISSION OF THE CHURCH

Some pastors keep track of a couple's anniversary, making a point to contact them on their first anniversary. Perhaps other church leaders, such as deacons, could take on this task as well, asking about the couple's well-being, inviting them to visit the church on a Sunday near their anniversary, and letting them know that the church will be praying for them as they mark a year of marriage.

Churches can do even more to uphold marriages as a part of their mission when couples are part of the congregation. More seasoned married couples might serve as mentors or sponsors for newly married couples, sharing meals and inviting them into conversation about the struggles of marriage as well as the joys and praying for or with them. One congregation periodically holds gatherings to strengthen marriages. At a "married within five years" party, couples bring their wedding photos and their stories to share at a gathering hosted by an older couple. Another party brings together couples who have been married for a long time to tell their stories and perhaps even share their struggles. In doing so, a church may communicate that as Christians, we are all in this together; we can support each other in remembering our vows, acknowledging our hardships, and upholding one another in love and prayer. Such relationships might end up being significant for couples who experience serious trouble in their marriage.

Convinced that couples need to prepare not only for marriage, but also for discipleship, Catholic liturgists Diana Macalintal and Nick Wagner suggest that couples go through a postwedding reflection. This could be done with a group of recently married people, between a couple and a pastor, or with a mentoring couple. First, the couple(s) close their eyes and think back over the day of their wedding. What was it like when they first saw the church? When they first saw each other? What do they remember about the moment when they made their vows or exchanged rings? What sorts of feelings did they have that day? After sharing their memories, they spend ten minutes in silence, thinking about the wedding service, noting what was most memorable. What did that moment say about God, or love, or promises? Another time of sharing follows. Finally, there is a time of study; choose a passage of Scripture that was read at the wedding or another text that sheds light on the Christian understanding of marriage (one of the texts suggested in chap. 4 would work well). Discuss how the text speaks to their life together. Close in prayer.[4]

Other ways of supporting couples in their marriages take place in worship. If a couple want to renew their vows, suggest they do so in the midst of a Sunday service, where the entire assembly can pray for them as well as celebrate with them. Or schedule a special service for the renewal of wedding vows at a time when a number of couples can reaffirm their commitment to one another. It is important to take care with such occasions, however, so that single, divorced, or widowed people do not feel excluded or unnecessarily pained.

Perhaps one of the most important thing a church can do is to include marriage in its ongoing discourse. Study the biblical texts we have named in this book. Talk theologically, not only therapeutically, about marriage. Speak openly about the reality of divorce (more on this below). Talk with children about what it looks like to care for others and discuss with youth how faith shapes loving relationships. When preaching about forgiveness, include marriage as one arena where that happens. When preaching about hospitality, point to the way it can be acted out in a marriage, and in a home, as a way of ingraining, ever more deeply, this essential Christian practice. When voicing the prayers of the people, mention those who struggle in their marriages or those who are in need of reconciliation. Whenever you speak a blessing, do it with conviction, for all God's children need to be assured that whatever befalls them, Christ is there.

WHEN DIVORCE HAPPENS

Even in the face of divorce statistics and dire predictions about the institution of marriage, people still stand up together and make promises. We continue to live in hope that it is possible to journey through life together with one other person who knows us intimately and loves us deeply. We keep holding out the possibility that we can keep the vows we make for a lifetime, until death do us part. We recognize that stable relationships are good for us and good for our society, and, at some deep level, we want to live and love with the same constancy and fidelity with which God loves us.

And yet we know from our own experience and that of others that it does not always work this way. People are, by nature, flawed creatures, and we do harm to one another, sometimes in ways that are irreparable. In the case of physical abuse, this harm is obvious; emotional abuse is more difficult to detect. Sometimes the harm comes from neglect, and sometimes a covenant simply cannot be kept any longer because something elemental has shifted and the capacity to love another as God intends has been irrevocably lost.

Divorce is painful for all involved—not just for the couple, but for everyone whose lives are connected to theirs. There is a tear in the social fabric when two people dissolve a marriage. As Christians who subscribe to the notions that reconciliation is to be desired, redemption is possible, and grace covers all, we seek to uphold marriages in whatever ways we can. And yet there are times when it seems evident that to maintain the shell of a marriage causes more harm than good. Ethicist Margaret Farley is eminently helpful here. She identifies three reasons that divorce is defensible:

> A commitment no longer binds when (1) it becomes *impossible* to keep; (2) it no longer fulfills any of the *purposes* it was meant to serve; (3) another obligation comes into *conflict* with the first obligation, and the second is judged to *override* the first. Only one of these conditions needs to be in place—although often more than one characterizes the situation—in order to justify a release from the commitment-obligation.[5]

Discerning these conditions is, to be sure, complex and

subjective, but these general categories help us look at human relationships with the eyes of grace. There are times when one partner has changed so utterly that she or he finds it impossible to maintain a relationship that is respectful and loving. Sometimes a marriage can no longer be sustained as the sphere in which partners can love and serve one another, or their communities, or God. At other times, obligations to God, or to one's children, or to the larger needs of the society interfere with the ability to maintain a marriage.[6]

Even when divorce is the only way forward, however, it remains incumbent upon partners to continue to love one another in the same way that a Christian is called to love all people. In fact, sometimes divorce is the only way that a person can continue to show love to someone they can no longer live with. Certainly when children are involved, parents must be diligent in treating one another with respect, if not affection, refraining from criticizing or blaming the other or competing for their children's loyalty.

To wonder *whether* marriage is indissoluble is to ask the wrong question. Marriages are dissolved all the time, sometimes in a courtroom, sometimes in the quiet desperation of a home. Even within a so-called intact marriage, covenants are broken, sometimes irreparably. The question is, then, how do we live as Christians, showing the love of God in all we do, even in the midst of brokenness? How does the church respond when all hope of fruitfulness is gone or when couples find that it is no longer possible to keep their vows within the bond of marriage?

These questions deserve far greater treatment than this book offers. The point is, however, that churches should respond to divorcing couples with love and prayer. Divorce is terrifying to the married; if it can happen to a couple you know, then maybe it can happen to you. And so we sometimes respond with judgment and are quick to create an environment of shame. But we can do better.

RITUALIZING DIVORCE

During the research phase of this book, people mentioned the need for a liturgy for divorce. It is difficult, indeed, to picture some couples, caught up in a swirl of fury, meeting peaceably to ritualize the end of their marriage. But possibilities for doing just this are gradually emerging.

A ritual for the time of divorce is not to be construed as a celebration of a breakup, nor is it a "blessing" of the divorce. Rather, it is an opportunity for two people to respectfully release one another from marriage vows, confessing sin and hearing assurances of forgiveness. It can create a space to pray for the partners as they cleave from one another and to pray for any children who will live a new kind of life. Sometimes, of course, a divorce is a life-saving measure for a spouse or for children, and involving both partners in this sort of ritual may not be possible. But when it is possible, it may serve as a time of redemption and healing and may provide the chance to make new promises, especially regarding the care and upbringing of children.

No divorce—not even the most amicable—is ever easy, and ritualizing divorce is a difficult thing to undertake. Yet it can be an opportunity to bring into the light what often remains hidden and to allow hurting couples to stand before God in prayer. Episcopal Bishop Gene Robinson describes movingly the ritual he and his wife undertook when they took a priest with them to the judge's chambers on the day of their divorce:

> After the divorce hearing, we followed the priest back to his parish and ended our marriage where it had begun: in church. There was no liturgy for the ending of a marriage, so far as we knew. So we made it up out of whole cloth, in the context of a Communion service. I felt sadder than I had ever felt in my life. So sad I could hardly breathe. At the time of the confession, I remember saying over and over, "I am so, so sorry." Indeed, each of us asked each other's forgiveness for what had happened. The prayers we prayed were for each other,

for healing from all this pain, and for our futures apart. And then, in the worst moment of all, heart-stoppingly painful, we prayed for our daughters—hoping against hope that we would not harm them too much in what we were about to do. With every ounce of commitment we could muster, we pledged ourselves to the joint raising and nurturing of our children. And then, in one of the holiest, and most healing moments of my life, we gave our wedding rings back to each other as the symbol of our wedding vows that we no longer held each other to. And then we shared the Body and Blood of Christ in a service of Holy Communion. I don't know if there was ever a time, before or since, when I was in such need of God's sustenance. I don't know how we did it, to be honest. It felt as exquisitely holy as it was excruciatingly painful. Somehow we had just managed to end our marriage in a loving way and not just slink away from God under cloak of night.[7]

Not every couple who divorces is able to do what Robinson and his spouse did. Yet his description helps to show how even in the face of one of the most painful experiences of life, God breaks in with the assurance of constant care, the Spirit enables us to speak truth in love, and Christ nourishes and sustains us with his own body that our brokenness might be mended.

Although the practice is not commonplace, a few resources are available to guide those interested in developing rituals for divorce. The United Church of Christ's *Book of Worship* includes an Order for Recognition of the End of Marriage, to be used when a couple wants to "acknowledge responsibility for their separation, affirm the good that continues from the previous relationship, and promise in the presence of God, family, and supportive friends to begin a new relationship." It is noted that whatever promises are made should be carefully determined by the couple. The opening sentences reflect the need for Christ's presence and God's continuing care through a time of turmoil. The prayers include thanksgiving for the relationship and supplication for healing. After the reading of Scripture, the divorcing partners may speak words of regret or confession, offer affirmations of mutual respect, or make promises to support and care for their children.[8]

An Anglican service for the end of a marriage acknowledges the sadness involved, provides an opportunity for confession and the assurance of forgiveness, and includes the reading of Scripture. In this service, two people take part in the Undoing of the Vows, in which each person releases the other from the marriage vow, thanks the other for the love and support given throughout the marriage, and asks forgiveness for his or her part in the failure of the marriage. Afterward, they return their rings to one another; the celebrant places the rings on the altar to signify that their lives are encompassed by the love and mercy of God.[9] In situations where only one person is willing or able to participate in some sort of ritual at the time of divorce, consider adapting a service of healing and wholeness, that she or he might have the opportunity to be lifted up in prayer.

MARRIAGE, MISSION, AND ESCHATOLOGICAL HOPE

It may seem strange to close a book about marriage with a discussion of ways to end it. And yet in doing so we find ourselves at the heart of this work: the entirety of our lives—our loves, our faith, our commitments, our dreams—is rooted in eschatological hope. We make promises to one another that express our conviction that the love of God, who intends to bring to completion a world of justice, peace, and unending joy, is the spring from which our own love is fed. And when we face the anguish of heartbreak, we continue to live into that vision of what God intends for the world, trusting in the grace of Christ to cover us and the love of God to sustain us. We do not give up hope, even when all the signs would convince us otherwise; we do not live in despair. There is a mercy that covers all of our mistakes—our omissions, our betrayals, the wounds we inflict.

There is a mercy whose light extinguishes all that threatens to undo us, a grace that infuses even the coldest, darkest corners of our hearts with warmth. When all is said and done, there is no failure too great, no sin too deep, that cannot be obliterated by the shock of the enormity of God's love.

The church is surely changing, and we are called to be increasingly creative about how we proclaim this good news as we worship in coffee shops and preside at weddings on sugar sand beaches. Whether we find ourselves standing in a pulpit worn smooth by a century's worth of hands or seated on a stool in the corner of a bistro, at the heart of the church's mission is the proclamation of that hope and the living out of the reign of God, here and now. In baptism and Eucharist we enact God's realm of justice and peace. We shape our prayers to the contours of the kingdom. And when we marry—or accompany others on their journeys of marriage—we do so as citizens of a heavenly country, rehearsing, in our own faltering way, for the wedding banquet we will enjoy when we are called home, shining with the glory of God, whose deepest desire is to unite us all.

Appendix A

SCRIPTURE READINGS
FOR WEDDINGS

OLD TESTAMENT

Ruth 1:16–17

1 Samuel 18:1–4; 20:16–17

Ecclesiastes 4:9–12

Song of Songs 2:10–13

Song of Songs 7:6–13

Song of Songs 8:6–7

PSALMS

Psalm 100

Psalm 105:1–6

EPISTLES

Romans 12:9–18

1 Corinthians 13:1–13

Galatians 5:14, 22–26

Ephesians 3:14–21

Philippians 2:1–13

Colossians 3:12–17

1 John 3:18–24

1 John 4:7–16

GOSPELS

Matthew 5:13–16

Mark 12:28–34

Luke 6:37–38

John 2:1–11

John 15:9–17

Appendix B

HYMNS FOR WEDDINGS

CLASSIC HYMNS

"Beloved, God's Chosen"
"Come, My Way, My Truth, My Life"
"Come, Thou Fount of Every Blessing"
"Deck Yourself, My Soul, with Gladness"
"Jesus, Come! For We Invite You"
"Joyful, Joyful, We Adore Thee"
"Love Divine, All Loves Excelling"
"More Love to Thee, O Christ"
"Now Thank We All Our God"
"O Love That Wilt Not Let Me Go"
"O Morning Star, How Fair and Bright"
"Praise the Lord! God's Glories Show"

CONTEMPORARY HYMNS

"Although I Speak with Angel's Tongue"
"A Hymn in Praise of God's Love"*
"Rejoice in Christ the Lord! (In Love Abide)"*
"From Sacred Love"
"Love Has Brought Us Here Together"

*Published in Kimberly Bracken Long and David Maxwell, eds., *Inclusive Marriage Services: A Wedding Sourcebook* (Louisville, KY: Westminster John Knox Press, 2015).

NOTES

Chapter 1: The State of the Union

1. Hunter Schwarz, "For the First Time, There Are More Single American Adults Than Married Ones, and Here's Where They Live," *Washington Post*, September 15, 2014, http://www.washingtonpost.com/blogs/govbeat/wp/2014/09/15/for-the-first-time-there-are-more-single-american-adults-than-married-ones-and-heres-where-they-live/.
2. Stephanie Coontz, "The Disestablishment of Marriage," *New York Times*, June 22, 2013, http://www.nytimes.com/2013/06/23/opinion/sunday/coontz-the-disestablishment-of-marriage.html?pagewanted=all&_r=0.
3. Ibid.
4. Ibid.
5. W. Hodding Carter, "Good Dog," *Garden and Gun* (October–November 2014): 87.
6. Cf. Mark Earey, *Worship That Cares: An Introduction to Pastoral Liturgy* (London: SCM Press, 2012), 99.
7. Coontz, "Disestablishment of Marriage."
8. Lauren Fox, "The Science of Cohabitation: A Step toward Marriage, Not a Rebellion," *Atlantic,* March 20, 2014, http://www.theatlantic.com/health/archive/2014/03/the-science-of-cohabitation-a-step-toward-marriage-not-a-rebellion/284512/.
9. Richard Fry, "New Census Data Show More Americans Are Tying the Knot, but Mostly It's the College-Educated," Pew Research Center, February 6, 2014, http://www.pewresearch.org/fact-tank/2014/02/06/new-census-data-show-more-americans-are-tying-the-knot-but-its-the-college-educated.
10. Andrew L. Yarrow, "Falling Marriage Rates Reveal Economic Fault Lines," *New York Times*, February 8, 2015,

http://www.nytimes.com/2015/02/08/fashion/weddings/falling-marriage-rates-reveal-economic-fault-lines.

11. June Carbone and Naomi Cahn, *Marriage Markets: How Inequality Is Remaking the American Family* (New York: Oxford University Press, 2014), 3–4.

12. Carbone and Cahn, *Marriage Markets*, 2–3.

13. Michael Brendan Dougherty, "Sorry *New York Times*: The State of Marriage Is Not Good," December 4, 2014, http://theweek.com/articles/441778/sorry-new-york-times-state-marriage-america-not-good.

14. Stephanie Coontz and Nancy Folbre, "Marriage, Poverty, and Public Policy" (discussion paper, Council on Contemporary Families, Fifth Annual CCF Conference, April 26–28, 2002), http://www.pbs.org/wgbh/pages/frontline/shows/marriage/etc/poverty.html.

15. Ibid.

16. Ralph Richard Banks, *Is Marriage for White People? How the African American Marriage Decline Affects Everyone* (New York: Plume, 2012), 3.

17. Paul Taylor, Jeffrey S. Passel, Wendy Wang, and Gabriel Velasco, "For Millennials, Parenthood Trumps Marriage," Pew Social and Demographic Trends, March 9, 2011, http://www.pewsocialtrends.org/files/2011/03/millennials-marriage.pdf, 1.

18. Ibid., 2.

19. Ibid., 3.

20. Pamela Paul, *The Starter Marriage and the Future of Matrimony* (New York: Random House, 2002), xv.

21. Ibid., 5–6.

22. See, for example, Sascha Rothchild, "The Case for the Starter Marriage," *Huffington Post*, posted November 9, 2010, and updated May 25, 2011.

23. Caryle Murphy, "Interfaith Marriage Is Common in U.S., Particularly among the Recently Wed," Pew Research Center, June 2, 2015, http://www.pewresearch.org/fact-tank/2015/06/02/interfaith-marriage/.

24. Wendy Wang, "The Rise of Intermarriage," Pew Research Center, February 16, 2012, http://www.pewsocialtrends.org/2012/02/16/the-rise-of-intermarriage/.

25. Andrew J. Cherlin, *The Marriage-Go-Round: The State of Marriage and the Family in America Today* (New York: Vintage Books, 2009), 4.

26. Christopher Ingraham, "Divorce Is Actually on the Rise, and It's the Baby Boomers' Fault," *Washington Post,* March 3, 2014, http://www.washingtonpost.com/blogs/wonkblog/wp/2014/03/27/divorce-is-actually-on-the-rise-and-its-the-baby-boomers-fault/.

27. Eli J. Finkel, "The All-or-Nothing Marriage," *New York Times*, February 14, 2014, http://www.nytimes.com/2014/02/15/opinion/sunday/the-all-or-nothing-marriage.html?_r=0.

28. Ibid.

29. Samantha Stark, "Vows," *New York Times*, October 19, 2013, http://www.nytimes.com/interactive/2014/fashion/weddings/vows-of-love.html?ref=weddings.

30. Thomas Geyer, "Two Q-C Women Marry after 72 Years Together," *Quad-City Times*, September 8, 2014, http://qctimes.com/news/local/q-c-women-marry-after-years-together/article_e350e94e-4eb4-551b-ad6a-d84092f7ec3f.html.

31. Rosemary Joyce, "Ask an Anthropologist about Marriage," *Psychology Today,* March 27, 2013, http://www.psychologytoday.com/blog/what-makes-us-human/201303/ask-anthropologist-about-marriage.

32. Ibid.

33. Stephanie Coontz, *Marriage, a History: How Love Conquered Marriage* (New York: Penguin Books, 2006), 1.

34. John Witte Jr., *From Sacrament to Contract: Marriage, Religion, and Law in the Western Tradition*, 2nd ed. (Louisville, KY: Westminster John Knox Press, 2012), 183.

35. Ibid., 199.

36. Coontz, *Marriage, a History,* 1.

37. See, for example, William Stacy Johnson, *A Time to Embrace: Same-Sex Relationships in Religion, Law, and Politics,* 2nd ed. (Grand Rapids: William B. Eerdmans Publishing Co., 2012); James V. Brownson, *Bible, Gender, Sexuality: Reframing the Church's Debate on Same-Sex Relationships* (Grand Rapids: William B. Eerdmans Publishing Co., 2013); Mark Achtemeier, *The Bible's Yes to Same-Sex Marriage* (Louisville, KY: Westminster John Knox Press, 2014).

38. Margaret A. Farley, *Just Love: A Framework for Christian Sexual Ethics* (New York: Continuum International Publishing Group, 2006), 269.

39. Cheryll Ann Cody, "Marriage," in *Dictionary of Afro-American Slavery,* ed. Randall M. Miller and John David Smith (New York: Greenwood Press, 1988).

Chapter 2: Should the Church Get Out of the Wedding Business?

1. The title appears on the Web site of A Little White Wedding Chapel. See http://www.alittlewhitechapel.com/chapel -history/charolette-story/.
2. The chapel's Web site explains that the drive-through service is a result of Ms. Richards seeing a disabled couple having trouble exiting their car, http://www.alittlewhitechapel.com/ fivechapels/tunnel-of-love-drive-thru/.
3. Rebecca Mead, *One Perfect Day: The Selling of the American Wedding* (New York: Penguin Books, 2007), 219.
4. Ibid., 221.
5. Ibid., 221–22.
6. Maryann Rohrlich, "When the 'Aisle' Is Slippery and Buggy," *New York Times*, September 21, 2012, http://www.nytimes .com/2012/09/23/fashion/weddings/summer-camps-as -destination-weddings.html?_r=0.
7. Thank you to Claudia Aguílar Rubalcava for telling me about her own wedding in Mexico City.
8. Kathryn Vasel, "Couples Now Spend More Than $30,000 to Get Married," *CNN Money*, March 12, 2015, http://money .cnn.com/2015/03/12/pf/planning-for-wedding-costs/.
9. "Wedding Industry: 5 Sectors That Will Profit from Increased Nuptial Spending," *Huffington Post*, April 2, 2013, http://www .huffingtonpost.com/2013/04/02/wedding-industry_n _3002354.html.
10. These are the prominent features on The Knot on October 28, 2012. See www.theknot.com.
11. Mead, *One Perfect Day*, 68.
12. Ibid., 69.
13. Ibid., 9.
14. Ibid.
15. See the Affirmation of the Families and the Affirmation of the Congregation in the marriage service of the Presbyterian Church (U.S.A.), in *The Book of Common Worship* (Louisville, KY: Westminster/John Knox Press, 1993).
16. Monica Wood, *Any Bitter Thing* (New York: Ballantine Books, 2006), 92–94.
17. B. J. Hutto, "Why a Church Wedding," *Christian Century* (May 28, 2015): 22.
18. Ibid.

19. Cherry Neill, letter to the editor, *Christian Century* (July 9, 2014): 6.
20. The International Anglican Liturgical Consultation, *Rites Relating to Marriage: A Statement and Resources from the International Anglican Liturgical Consultation, Auckland 2009– Canterbury 2011,* 1.14.
21. Ibid., 2.2.
22. Margaret A. Farley, *Just Love: A Framework for Christian Sexual Ethics* (New York: Continuum International Publishing Group, 2006), 263.

Chapter 3: What's Love Got to Do with It?

1. Stephanie Coontz, *Marriage, a History: How Love Conquered Marriage* (New York: Penguin Books, 2006), 5.
2. Ibid., 6.
3. Ibid., 78.
4. Ibid., 81.
5. Ibid., 89.
6. Ibid., 6.
7. Judith M. Bennett, "The Tie That Binds: Peasant Marriages and Families in Late Medieval England," *Journal of Interdisciplinary History* 15, no. 1 (1984): 111–29.
8. Andreas Capellanus, *The Art of Courtly Love*, ed. John Jay Parry (New York: Columbia University Press, 1941), 100. Quoted in David Shumway, *Modern Love: Romance, Intimacy, and the Marriage Crisis* (New York: New York University Press, 2003), 14. Shumway allows that the beginning of *The Art of Courtly Love* may have been a "hoax," since it eventually disapproves of extramarital love.
9. Marilyn Yalom, *How the French Invented Love: Nine Hundred Years of Passion and Romance* (New York: Harper Perennial, 2012), 14–15.
10. Ibid., 33.
11. Ibid., 37–38.
12. Coontz, *Marriage, a History*, 6.
13. Ibid., 7.
14. Ibid., 9.
15. Ibid., 7.
16. Ibid., 19.
17. Shannon McSheffrey, *Marriage, Sex, and Civic Culture in Late*

Medieval London (Philadelphia: University of Pennsylvania Press, 2006), 18–19.

18. Ibid., 19.
19. Belden C. Lane, *Ravished by Beauty: The Surprising Legacy of Reformed Spirituality* (New York: Oxford University Press, 2011), 107–8.
20. Anne Bradstreet, "A Letter to Her Husband, Absent upon Publick Employment," quoted in Wilson Yates, "The Protestant View of Marriage," in *Perspectives on Marriage: A Reader*, ed. Kieran Scott and Michael Warren, 3rd ed. (New York: Oxford University Press, 2007), 447.
21. Coontz, *Marriage, a History*, 138.
22. Ibid., 178.
23. Ibid., 146.
24. Ibid., 146–47.
25. Ibid., 177.
26. Marilyn Yalom, *A History of the Wife* (New York: Harper Collins, 2001), 242.
27. Ibid., 245.
28. Ibid., 226.
29. Coontz, *Marriage, a History*, 178.
30. Ibid., 185.
31. Ibid., 179–80.
32. Yalom, *History of the Wife,* 259.
33. Coontz, *Marriage, a History*, 189–90.
34. Shumway, *Modern Love*, 69.
35. Coontz, *Marriage, a History*, 200.
36. Ibid., 201.
37. George Bernard Shaw, *Getting Married: The Original Classic*, George Bernard Shaw Masterpiece Collection, 22. Available through CreateSpace Independent Publishing Platform, 2015.
38. Coontz, *Marriage, a History,* 202, 203 (emphasis added).
39. Ibid., 214.
40. David Croteau and William Hoynes, *Media / Society: Industries, Images and Audiences*, 5th ed. (Los Angeles: SAGE Publications, 2014), 172.
41. Coontz, *Marriage, a History*, 247.
42. Ibid., 278.
43. E. J. Graff, *What Is Marriage For? The Strange Social History of Our Most Intimate Institution* (Boston: Beacon Press, 2004), 2.
44. Stephanie Coontz, presentation at PopTech, https://www

.youtube.com/watch?v=6JPAn9tDnfE. Cf. Coontz, *Marriage, a History,* 309.

45. Richard B. Hays, *First Corinthians,* Interpretation commentary series (Louisville, KY: Westminster John Knox Press, 2011), 112.

46. Gordon D. Fee, *The First Epistle to the Corinthians,* rev. ed., New International Commentary on the New Testament (Grand Rapids: William B. Eerdmans Publishing Co., 2014), 317.

47. Tertullian, "To His Wife," in *Treatises on Marriage and Remarriage,* trans. William P. Le Saint, Ancient Christian Writers 13 (New York: Paulist Press, 1951), 35–36.

48. Geoffrey D. Dunn, *Tertullian,* Early Church Fathers (London: Routledge, 2004), 3.

49. David G. Hunter, *Marriage in the Early Church* (Eugene, OR: Wipf & Stock, 2001), 33–34. Originally published by Augsburg Fortress, 1992.

50. Ibid., 10–11.

51. Ibid., 34–35.

52. David Rankin, *Tertullian and the Church* (Cambridge: Cambridge University Press, 2007), 97.

53. Hunter, *Marriage in the Early Church,* 12–15.

54. Ibid., 18–21.

55. Hunter, *Marriage in the Early Church,* 102; Witte, *From Sacrament to Contract,* 68.

56. Quoted in Hunter, *Marriage in the Early Church,*104.

57. Ibid., 23.

58. Quoted in ibid., 108.

59. Philip L. Reynolds, *How Marriage Became One of the Sacraments: The Sacramental Theology of Marriage from Its Emergence to the Council of Trent* (Cambridge: Cambridge University Press, 2016), 242. Reynolds explains that Jovinian, Julian of Eclanum, and Ambrosiaster were among those who saw procreation in marriage as "part of the original, God-given order of things."

60. Hunter, *Marriage in the Early Church,* 109.

61. Saint Augustine, *Marriage and Virginity,* ed. David G. Hunter, trans. Ray Kearney, Works of Saint Augustine: A Translation for the 21st Century, pt. 1, vol. 9 (Hyde Park, NY: New City Press, 1999), 57.

62. Peter Brown, *The Body and Society: Men, Women, and Sexual Renunciation in Early Christianity* (New York: Columbia University Press, 1988), 403.

63. Reynolds, *How Marriage Became One of the Sacraments*, 416.

64. Ibid., 418.

65. Reynolds (ibid., 419) puts it this way: "The Western conception of marriage was not as rich as it might have been. As befitted an outsider's view, it did little to illumine the phenomenology of the married life. . . . The essence of a marriage, from this point of view, was in effect the unavailability of another marriage. . . . The fifth chapter of Ephesians depicted in outline a spirituality of the married life. It said nothing about indissolubility. . . . By identifying the 'sacramentality' of marriage with indissolubility, Augustine obscured the teaching of Ephesians."

66. Hunter, *Marriage in the Early Church*, 27. Some scholars consider Tertullian's mention of "that marriage which the church unites, the offering strengthens, the blessing seals, the angels proclaim, and the Father declares valid" as evidence of an early Christian marriage liturgy. A few late-fourth- and early-fifth-century documents refer to nuptial blessings, and a marriage poem (epithalamium) by Paulinus of Nola implies some sort of marriage ceremony in a church.

67. Hippolytus sternly criticized Callistus, the bishop of Rome (218–223 CE), for the church's practice of acknowledging marriages that were not according to the law. See "The Refutation of All Heresies," in *The Ante-Nicene Fathers*, vol. 5, ed. Alexander Roberts and James Donaldson, rev. A. Cleveland Coxe (Peabody, MA: Hendrickson Publishers, 1999), 131.

68. Mark Searle and Kenneth W. Stevenson, *Documents of the Marriage Liturgy* (Collegeville, MN: Liturgical Press, 1992), 253–54.

69. Ibid., 40–44.

70. Ibid., 43.

71. Ibid., 46.

72. Ibid., 47–48.

73. Ibid., 45.

74. Ibid., 121, 123.

75. These rubrics are quoted in ibid., 125.

76. Ibid., 12; Witte, *From Sacrament to Contract*, 91.

77. Searle and Stevenson, *Documents of the Marriage Liturgy*, 151.

78. Ibid., 152.

79. Ibid., 154–55.

80. Ibid., 12.
81. Peter Lombard, *Sentences,* 4.27.3, quoted in Searle and Stevenson, *Documents of the Marriage Liturgy*, 148–49.
82. Witte, *From Sacrament to Contract*, 93–94.
83. Ibid., 95.
84. Ibid., 96.
85. I am grateful to Philip Reynolds for sharing these insights, which are expressed in the first chapter of his book *How Marriage Became One of the Sacraments*.
86. Searle and Stevenson, *Documents of the Marriage Liturgy,* 158–62.
87. Ibid., 165–66. I have modernized the English spelling for ease of reading.
88. Ibid., 167–78.
89. Kenneth Stevenson, "Worship by the Book," in *The Oxford Guide to the Book of Common Prayer: A Worldwide Survey*, ed. Charles Hefling and Cynthia Shattuck (New York: Oxford University Press, 2006), 15.
90. Witte, *From Sacrament to Contract*, 5–6.
91. Ibid., 131.
92. Ibid., 123–24.
93. Searle and Stevenson, *Documents of the Marriage Liturgy*, 211.
94. Ibid., 212–14.
95. Witte, *From Sacrament to Contract*, 6.
96. Ibid.
97. Ibid., 159.
98. John Calvin, *Institutes of the Christian Religion* 1.19, 1.22; trans. Ford Lewis Battles (Atlanta: John Knox Press, 1975); quoted in Witte, *From Sacrament to Contract*, 165.
99. From Calvin's sermon on Eph. 5:22–26, 31–33, quoted in Witte, *From Sacrament to Contract*, 186.
100. Witte, *From Sacrament to Contract*, 7–8, 186.
101. John Witte Jr. and Robert M. Kingdon, *Sex, Marriage, and Family in John Calvin's Geneva*, vol. 1, *Courtship, Engagement, and Marriage* (Grand Rapids: William B. Eerdmans Publishing Co., 2005), 445.
102. Witte, *From Sacrament to Contract*, 187.
103. Ibid., 201–2. Witte is quoting from Calvin's commentaries on 1 Cor. 6:15–20 and Gen. 29:18.
104. Ibid., 200–204.
105. *The Parisian Passwind, Observations of Genevan Weddings* (1556), quoted in Witte, *From Sacrament to Contract*, 464.

106. Witte and Kingdon, *Sex, Marriage, and Family*, 448 n. 12.
107. John Calvin, *The Manner of Celebrating Holy Matrimony* (1545), in *Ioannis Calvini opera quae supersunt omnia*, ed. G. Baum et al. (Brunswick: C. A. Schwetschke & Filium, 1892), 6:203–8, quoted in Witte and Kingdon, *Sex, Marriage, and Family*, 465.
108. Calvin, *Manner of Celebrating Holy Matrimony*, quoted in Witte and Kingdon, *Sex, Marriage, and Family*, 466–67.
109. Witte and Kingdon, *Sex, Marriage, and Family*, 450.
110. Ibid., 452.
111. Ibid., 451–52.
112. Witte, *From Sacrament to Contract*, 179–80.
113. Ibid., 208.
114. The following summary of the marital history of Henry VIII is drawn from ibid., 221–26.
115. Searle and Stevenson, *Documents of the Marriage Liturgy*, 216–17. I have modernized the English spelling for easier reading.
116. Ibid., 217.
117. Ibid., 217–25.
118. Gillian Varcoe, "Marriage," in Hefling and Shattuck, *Oxford Guide to the Book of Common Prayer*, 511.
119. Witte, *From Sacrament to Contract*, 239–40.
120. Ibid., 240–41.
121. Ibid., 218–19.
122. Ibid., 219.
123. Ibid., 221.
124. William P. Roberts, "Christian Marriage," in *From Trent to Vatican II*, ed. Raymond F. Bulman and Frederick J. Parella (New York: Oxford University Press, 2006), 210.
125. Reynolds, *How Marriage Became One of the Sacraments*, 6.
126. Witte, *From Sacrament to Contract*, 92.
127. Roberts, "Christian Marriage," 210.
128. Kenneth W. Stevenson, *To Join Together: The Rite of Marriage* (New York: Pueblo Publishing Co., 1987), 50–51.
129. Witte, *From Sacrament to Contract*, 109.
130. Ibid.
131. Stevenson, *To Join Together*, 50–52.
132. Roberts, "Christian Marriage," 211. It should be noted that some changes were made to canon law in 1917.
133. Witte, *From Sacrament to Contract*, 10.
134. Ibid., 10–11.
135. Ibid., 10.

136. Margaret A. Farley, *Just Love: A Framework for Christian Sexual Ethics* (New York: Continuum International Publishing Group, 2006), 299–300.

Chapter 4: Feasting at the Table of Love

1. Ellen F. Davis, "The Soil That Is Scripture," in *Engaging Biblical Authority: Perspectives on the Bible as Scripture,* ed. William P. Brown (Louisville, KY: Westminster John Knox Press, 2007), 39.
2. Ibid.
3. John Burgess, *Why Scripture Matters: Reading the Bible in a Time of Church Conflict* (Louisville, KY: Westminster John Knox Press, 1998), 76.
4. Shirley C. Guthrie Jr., *Always Being Reformed: Faith for a Fragmented World,* 2nd ed. (Louisville, KY: Westminster John Knox Press, 2008), 21.
5. Margaret A. Farley, *Just Love: A Framework for Christian Sexual Ethics* (New York: Continuum International Publishing Group, 2006), 227.
6. Ibid., 228.
7. Mercy Amba Oduyoye, "A Coming Home to Myself," in *Liberating Eschatology: Essays in Honor of Letty M. Russell,* ed. Margaret Farley and Serene Jones (Louisville, KY: Westminster John Knox Press, 1999), 118. I am grateful to Amy Plantinga Pauw for acquainting me with this source.
8. *Celebrate God's Presence: A Book of Services for the United Church of Canada* (Etobicoke, ON: United Church Publishing House, 2000), 395.
9. William P. Brown, *The Seven Pillars of Creation: The Bible, Science, and the Ecology of Wonder* (New York: Oxford University Press, 2010), 8.
10. *Encyclopedia of the Bible and Its Reception, Vol. 11,* ed. Christine Helmer, Steven Linn Mckenzie, Thomas Chr. Römer, Jens Schröter, Barry Dov Walfish, and Eric Ziolkowski (Berlin: De Gruyter, 2015), 802.
11. Walter Brueggemann, "Of the Same Flesh and Bone (Gn 2,23a)," *Catholic Biblical Quarterly* 32 (1970): 535.
12. Ibid., 539–40.
13. John Goldingay, "Covenant, OT and NT," in *The New Interpreter's Dictionary of the Bible* (Nashville: Abingdon Press, 2006), 1:778.

14. Terence E. Fretheim, "The Book of Genesis: Introduction, Commentary, and Reflections," in *The New Interpreter's Bible*, vol. 1 (Nashville: Abingdon Press, 1994), 354.
15. Ibid.; Brueggemann, "Same Flesh and Bone," 540.
16. Brueggemann, "Same Flesh and Bone," 542.
17. Patrick Miller, "What Does Genesis 1–3 Teach about Sexuality, and How Should We Live in Response?" in *Frequently Asked Questions about Sexuality, the Bible, and the Church: Plain Talk about Tough Issues*, ed. Ted A. Smith (Kansas City, MO: Covenant Network of Presbyterians, 2006), 5. Thank you to Amy Plantinga Pauw for pointing me to these sources.
18. Farley, *Just Love*, 267.
19. Adrian Thatcher, *Marriage after Modernity: Christian Marriage in Postmodern Times* (New York: New York University Press, 1998), 95.
20. Brian Ellison, "Marriage Matters . . . Why?" (sermon preached at a conference of the Covenant Network of Presbyterians, Chicago, November 2, 2013).
21. Ibid.
22. Kathleen Norris, *The Cloister Walk* (New York: Riverhead Books, 1996), 261.
23. Ibid.
24. Sarah Coakley, "Pleasure Principles: Toward a Contemporary Theology of Desire," *Harvard Divinity Bulletin* (2005): 27. Quoted in David H. Jensen, *God, Desire, and a Theology of Human Sexuality* (Louisville, KY: Westminster John Knox Press, 2013), 108.
25. Ellison, "Marriage Matters . . . Why?"
26. Luise Schottroff has noted that the exhortations to husbands in Ephesians 5 are not terribly different from the writings of pagan authors who take care to describe the role of father and husband as different from that of the authoritarian tyrant. See Luise Schottroff, *Lydia's Impatient Sisters: A Feminist Social History of Early Christianity* (Louisville, KY: Westminster John Knox Press, 1995), 22–33. Noted in Ian McFarland, "A Canonical Reading of Ephesians 5:21–33: Theological Gleanings," *Theology Today* 57 (October 2000): 347 n. 10.
27. Frances Taylor Gench, *Encountering God in Tyrannical Texts: Reflections on Paul, Women, and the Authority of Scripture* (Louisville, KY: Westminster John Knox Press, 2015), 30.

28. E. Elizabeth Johnson, "Ephesians," in *Women's Bible Commentary,* 3rd ed., ed. Carol A. Newsom, Sharon H. Ringe, and Jacqueline E. Lapsley (Louisville, KY: Westminster John Knox Press, 2012), 586.

29. McFarland, "Canonical Reading," 353.

30. Brueggemann, "Same Flesh and Bone," 541.

31. Johnson, "Ephesians," 579.

32. Thatcher, *Marriage after Modernity*, 37.

33. Craig S. Keener, *The Gospel of Matthew: A Socio-Rhetorical Commentary* (Grand Rapids: William B. Eerdmans Publishing Co., 2009), 463.

34. *Evangelical Lutheran Worship, Leader's Desk Edition* (Minneapolis: Augsburg Fortress, 2006), 678.

35. Kimberly L. Clayton, "God's Beloved—Known for Our Parties?" (sermon preached at the Presbyterian Association of Musicians Worship and Music Conference, Montreat, NC, June 2015).

36. Mark Searle, untitled paragraph in *A Marriage Sourcebook*, ed. J. Robert Baker, Joni Reiff Gibley, and Kevin Charles Gibley (Chicago: Liturgy Training Publications, 1994), 103.

37. Standing Commission on Liturgy and Music, *I Will Bless You and You Will Be a Blessing: Resources for the Witnessing and Blessing of a Lifelong Covenant in a Same-Sex Relationship* (New York: Church Publishing, 2012), Kindle version, loc. 258 of 2901.

38. An Outline of the Faith, in *The Book of Common Prayer and Administration of the Sacraments and Other Rites and Ceremonies of the Church, together with the Psalter or Psalms of David according to the Use of the Episcopal Church* (New York: Church Hymnal Corp., 1979), 855.

39. Standing Commission on Liturgy and Music, *I Will Bless You*, loc. 258 of 2901.

40. Jean Vanier, *Essential Writings*, ed. Carolyn Whitney-Brown (Maryknoll, NY: Orbis Books, 2008), 93–94.

41. Corrie ten Boom, *The Hiding Place* (New York: Bantam Books, 1984), 238.

42. Martin Luther King Jr., *Strength to Love* (Minneapolis: Fortress Press, 2010), 45.

43. *Book of Common Prayer*, 429.

44. Mark Searle and Kenneth W. Stevenson, *Documents of the Marriage Liturgy* (Collegeville, MN: Liturgical Press, 1992), 266.

45. Ibid., 271.
46. *Book of Common Prayer,* 429.
47. See, for example, J. Cheryl Exum, *Song of Songs,* Old Testament Library (Louisville, KY: Westminster John Knox Press, 2005), 1.
48. *Jerry Maguire,* directed by Cameron Crowe (Culver City, CA: TriStar Pictures, 1996).
49. Johnson, "Ephesians," 579.
50. McFarland, "Canonical Reading," 356.
51. Brian K. Blount, *Revelation: A Commentary,* New Testament Library (Louisville, KY: Westminster John Knox Press, 2009), 380.
52. Ibid., 381.
53. Wendell Berry, "The Body and the Earth," in *The Art of the Commonplace: The Agrarian Essays of Wendell Berry,* ed. Norman Wirzba (Berkeley, CA: Counterpoint, 2002), 112–13.
54. Norris, *Cloister Walk,* 22.
55. Berry, "Body and Earth," 117.
56. Farley, *Just Love,* 68.

Chapter 5: The Christian Wedding

1. Courtney E. Martin, "An Unofficial Guide to Officiating a Wedding of 'Nones,'" *On Being,* January 23, 2015, http://www.onbeing.org/blog/an-unofficial-guide-to-officiating-a-wedding-of-nones/7236.
2. According to its Web site, the Universal Life Church has ordained more than twenty million ministers around the world. http://www.themonastery.org/ordination?gclid=CjOKEQjw9o-vBRCO0OLi2PfPkI8BEiQA8pdF4LZGNvshIQYThLucReZxqX8SL8–JlokRW9xkJCcUdSAaAmbh8P8HAQ.
3. Martin, "Wedding of 'Nones.'"
4. David Maxwell, "My Big Fat Gay Wedding," Ecclesio.com, February 8, 2013, http://www.ecclesio.com/2013/02/my-big-fat-gay-wedding-david-maxwell/#sthash.T7RjLWSJ.dpuf.
5. Kenneth W. Stevenson, *To Join Together: The Rite of Marriage* (New York: Pueblo Publishing Co., 1987), 165.
6. *Respectful Presence: An Understanding of Interfaith Prayer and Celebration from a Reformed Christian Perspective,* a document from the Presbyterian Church (U.S.A.) 209th General Assembly (1997), par. 131. Available at https://www.pcusa.org/resource/respectful-presence-document/.

7. Kimberly Bracken Long and David Maxwell, eds., *Inclusive Marriage Services: A Wedding Sourcebook* (Louisville, KY: Westminster John Knox Press, 2015), 97–98. Several other statements on marriage can be found in this volume.

8. Standing Commission on Liturgy and Music, *Liturgical Resources 1: I Will Bless You and You Will Be a Blessing*, rev. ed. (New York: Church Publishing, 2015), 162.

9. Long and Maxwell, *Inclusive Marriage Services*, 103–4.

10. Ibid., 4.

11. *The Book of Common Worship* (Louisville, KY: Westminster/ John Knox Press, 1993), 843.

12. Standing Commission on Liturgy and Music, *I Will Bless You*, 164.

13. Ken Kovacs, "Dress You Up in My Love" (sermon preached at a regional conference of the Covenant Network of Presbyterians, Baton Rouge, Louisiana, January 24, 2015).

14. For further reflection on preaching at weddings, see Teresa Lockhart Stricklen, "How Can We Not Preach at Weddings? Combing the Contexts of the Rhetorical Situation for a Fit Word from the Lord," *Call to Worship: Liturgy, Music, Preaching, and the Arts* 41, no. 3 (2008): 29–37.

15. Bernard Cooke, "What God Has Joined Together . . . ," in *Perspectives on Marriage: A Reader*, ed. Kieran Scott and Michael Warren, 3rd ed. (New York: Oxford University Press, 2007), 349.

16. Kathleen Norris, *Acedia and Me: A Marriage, Monks, and a Writer's Life* (New York: Riverhead Books, 2008), 182.

17. Kathleen Hughes, *Saying Amen: A Mystagogy of Sacrament* (Chicago: Liturgy Training Publications, 2007), 106.

18. *Christian Marriage: The Worship of God*, Supplemental Liturgical Resource 3, prepared by the Office of Worship for the Presbyterian Church (U.S.A.) and the Cumberland Presbyterian Church (Philadelphia: Westminster Press, 1986), 94.

19. For a fuller discussion of this question, see "Couples with Children," in Long and Maxwell, *Inclusive Marriage Services*, 188–90.

20. Standing Commission on Liturgy and Music, *I Will Bless You*, 169.

21. See, for instance, Patrick W. O'Neil, "Bosses and Broomsticks: Ritual and Authority in Antebellum Slave Weddings," *Journal*

of Southern History 75, no. 1 (February 2009): 29–48. I am indebted to the Rev. John D. Menefee Jr. for pointing me to this research.

22. *Book of Common Worship*, 848.
23. Julie McCarty, "'Nuptial Pentecost': Theological Reflections on the Presence and Action of the Holy Spirit in Christian Marriage," in Scott and Warren, *Perspectives on Marriage*, 85.
24. Paul Evdokimov, *The Sacrament of Love: The Nuptial Mystery in the Light of the Orthodox Tradition*, trans. Anthony P. Gythiel and Victoria Steadman (Crestwood, NY: St. Vladimir's Seminary Press, 1995), 153.
25. McCarty, "'Nuptial Pentecost,'" 85.
26. *Evangelical Lutheran Worship*, Pew Edition (Minneapolis: Augsburg Fortress, 2006), 289.
27. McCarty, "'Nuptial Pentecost,'" 88–89.
28. Arlo D. Duba, "Take Me to the Water: Ideas for Keeping Baptism Front and Center," *Reformed Worship*, December 2001, http://www.reformedworship.org/article/december-2001/take-me-water-ideas-keeping-baptism-front-and-center.
29. Long and Maxwell, *Inclusive Marriage Services*, 146.
30. Prayer composed by David Gambrell for the 2015 Montreat Worship and Music Conference, Montreat, North Carolina.
31. Long and Maxwell, *Inclusive Marriage Services*, 6.
32. Ibid., 22.
33. *Book of Common Worship*, 851.
34. Herman G. Stuempfle Jr., "Unseen God, Your Hand Has Guided" (1998), text © 2000 GIA Publications Inc. This hymn can be found in the hymnal *Glory to God* (Louisville, KY: Westminster John Knox Press, 2013), 685.
35. Mary Louise Bringle, "Love Has Brought Us Here Together," text ©2009 GIA Publications. The text is set to the tune HYFRYDOL in *Gather*, 3rd ed. (Chicago: GIA Publications, 2010), 969. The text alone can be found in Long and Maxwell, *Inclusive Marriage Services*, 166.
36. The texts of both hymns are in Long and Maxwell, *Inclusive Marriage Services*, 162–64.
37. *Wedding and Funeral Music* is available as a booklet or a free PDF download at the Presbyterian Association of Musicians' Web site, www.PresbyMusic.org.
38. Adapted from "Some Questions to Address in a Session Marriage Policy," in *The Companion to the* Book of Common

Worship, ed. Peter C. Bower (Louisville, KY: Geneva Press, 2003), 230–31.

39. Adapted from "Suggestions for Conducting a Wedding Rehearsal," in Bower, *Companion to the* Book of Common Worship, 231–33.

Chapter 6: Marriage and the Church's Mission

1. Diana Macalintal and Nick Wagner, *Joined by the Church, Sealed By a Blessing: Couples and Communities Called to Conversion Together* (Collegeville, MN: Liturgical Press, 2014), 52.
2. Macalintal and Wagner suggest similar ideas, offering interpretations from a Roman Catholic perspective.
3. Julie McCarty, "'Nuptial Pentecost': Theological Reflections on the Presence and Action of the Holy Spirit in Christian Marriage," in *Perspectives on Marriage: A Reader*, ed. Kieran Scott and Michael Warren, 3rd ed. (New York: Oxford University Press, 2007), 84.
4. This idea is based on a postsacramental reflection described by Macalintal and Wagner, *Joined by the Church*, 125–28.
5. Margaret A. Farley, *Just Love: A Framework for Christian Sexual Ethics* (New York: Continuum International Publishing Group, 2006), 305.
6. Farley, *Just Love*, 306–7.
7. Gene Robinson, *God Believes in Love: Straight Talk about Gay Marriage* (New York: Vintage Books, 2013), 10–11.
8. An Order for the Recognition of the End of Marriage, in *United Church of Christ Book of Worship* (Cleveland, OH: United Church of Christ Office for Church Life and Leadership, 1986), 289–95.
9. "End of a Marriage (Anglican)," in Abigail Rian Evans, *Healing Liturgies for the Seasons of Life* (Louisville, KY: Westminster John Knox Press, 2004), 112–18.